Autobiography - And Other Funny Stories

Charles H. Huettner

Copyright © 2016 Charles H. Huettner

ISBN: 978-1-63491-869-5

All rights reserved. No part of this publication may be reproduced, stored in a retrieval system, or transmitted in any form or by any means, electronic, mechanical, recording or otherwise, without the prior written permission of the author.

Published by BookLocker.com, Inc., St. Petersburg, Florida.

Printed on acid-free paper.

BookLocker.com, Inc.
2016

First Edition

Acknowledgements

My sincerest gratitude goes to my parents Ruth and Henry Huettner for their generous love, support, and understanding, and for teaching me by example.

I thank my family, friends and associates for a rich and fulfilling life and for accomplishing what I have set out to achieve.

I praise the Holy Spirit for Your insights, protection, and blessings.

Also, in memory of my lifelong friend Tom Barnes and my pilot training buddy Bob Szul who died the day this book was sent to my publisher.

About the Author

Mr. Huettner is the Executive Director of the Aerospace States Association (ASA), which is comprised of Lt. Governors and delegates from the nation's 50 states. ASA works to establish national aerospace policy and enhance state aerospace education and economic development efforts. In addition, Mr. Huettner is the President of Charles Huettner Associates a consulting firm specializing in cross-government/industry aerospace strategies, problem solving, and coalition building.

Mr. Huettner retired after 33 years of government service as the Executive Director of the Presidential "Commission on the Future of the US Aerospace Industry". Prior to this, he was the Policy Advisor for Aviation for the National Science and Technology Council (NSTC), in the Executive Office of the President (SES-4). In that role, he was responsible for interagency coordination and implementation of the Administration's policies and programs related to aeronautics R&D; aviation safety, security, efficiency and environment; and GPS. During this period he initiated the development of a national aviation policy and led the effort to remove GPS Selective Availability that was signed by the President.

In 1997, Mr. Huettner negotiated the strategic alliance between FAA and NASA and served as the first Executive Secretary of the FAA/NASA Executive Committee, which was responsible for implementing the alliance. Mr. Huettner was also the Director for Aviation Safety Research at NASA where he initiated the development of NASA's half billion-dollar aviation safety research initiative. At FAA, he rose through the ranks from inspector to serve as the Deputy and Acting Associate Administrator for Aviation Safety.

In addition, Mr. Huettner has served on the White House Commission for Aviation Safety and Security, the National Civil Aviation Review Commission and coordinated the development of the National Science and Technology Council's "National Research Plan for Aviation Safety, Security, Efficiency and Environmental Compatibility". In 2005, he published the National Institute of Aerospace final report entitled <u>Responding to the Call: Aviation Plan for American Leadership</u>.

Mr. Huettner is an Airline Transport Pilot rated in the B-747, B-727 and the Air Force C-141 Starlifter, and has significant flight time in a wide range of business aircraft including the Gulfstream IV. Mr. Huettner has a Bachelor of Science Degree in Industrial Management from the University of Akron and a Masters Degree in Public Administration from Harvard's John F. Kennedy School of Government. He has a diploma in theological studies from the Virginia Theological Seminary and has written two books: <u>Jesus Reveals Revelation</u>, and <u>The Word & The Spirit: How God Speaks to YOU.</u>

Mr. Huettner retired as a Colonel in the USAF Reserves where he last served as the Reserve Augmentee to the Air Force Chief of Safety. His decorations include the Legion of Merit, Meritorious Service Medal, the Air Medal, the Air Force Commendation Medal, the Armed Forces Expeditionary Medal, the Combat Readiness Medal, and the Vietnam Service Medal.

He is a resident of Old Town Alexandria, VA, and is a former President of the Old Town Civic Association. He was elected Governor of the Old Dominion Boat Club.

TABLE OF CONTENTS

INTRODUCTION 1
CHAPTER 1: MT. LEBANON 3
CHAPTER 2: AKRON 27
CHAPTER 3: UASF 41
CHAPTER 4: HOME 77
CHAPTER 5: FAA 105
CHAPTER 6: B&B 145
CHAPTER 7: NASA 158
CHAPTER 8: WHITE HOUSE 165
EPILOGUE 189
END NOTES 221

INTRODUCTION

What do locking people in their house on trick night, the first Zippy, a dark room in Addis Ababa, Ethiopia, transforming airline pilot training, improving GPS, and Aviation Advisor at the White House on 9-11 have in common? They are all part of a long history of fascinating and often humorous stories in the life of Charles Huettner.

While this book is autobiographical it is not written to detail my life's story. I have written it at the urging of relatives, friends, and associates who found my true stories entertaining and urged me to write them down. This book contains episodes in an incredible life for your enjoyment and to learn a bit about how God and the government work from behind the scenes. You will get a glimpse of the humor and intrigue that I have experienced during 33 years in the USAF, FAA, NASA, and the White House and learn what it was like to grow up in Pittsburgh PA in the early1960s. You will read of my adventures while at Mt. Lebanon High School, the University of Akron, Harvard, Laredo Air Force Base (AFB), TX, McGuire AFB, NJ, the Pentagon and Old Town Alexandria. I have piloted a supersonic T-38 jet to 50,000 feet, flew a hot air balloon over Atlanta Hartsfield Airport during airline rush hour, experienced the transition between the Clinton and Bush Administrations in the White House, and toured the world with Buzz Aldrin, Neil deGrasse Tyson, and former House Science Committee Chairman Congressman Bob Walker. Come along with me to laugh and experience the amazing life of Charles Huettner.

Chapter 1: Mt. Lebanon

The old joke, I was born at an early age, was especially true for me. I was born very premature. I have had a rich life of experiences that have to some degree been formed from my being small, a 5'7" guy at my peak, and looking young for my age. In grade school, I was bullied, but made up for my lack of fighting ability by being bright, innovative, and energetic. My draft card at age 18 read 5 foot 75 pounds. There are hundreds of funny and amazing stories of things that have happened to me from my youth to working at the White House and beyond. I look forward to sharing some of them with you. I'll begin by telling you the story of "Cop Catching".

Cop Catching: Preemie-Infant care wasn't too advanced in 1946 when I was born. I am told that if it weren't for my nurse, Shirley Brown, feeding me with an eyedropper I would not have survived. I grew up at an idyllic time in history, the 1950s, in an idyllic place, Mt. Lebanon, a suburb of Pittsburgh, PA. The experience was right out of "Father Knows Best" and "Leave It To Beaver". Sure we had to worry about the USSR, and nuclear war, but the rest of the world was more or less at peace and prosperity had come to America after World War II. We were a middle class family living in an upper middle class community. My father, Henry, was an engineer and my mother, Ruth, was a homemaker. I am an only child, but there were lots of kids of all ages on our block.

My mother didn't drive until she was nearly 50 but we could walk two blocks to a little strip of local stores that included two drug stores, an A&P grocery store, an Isaly's ice cream parlor, Whitman's 5&10, Burt's gift shop, a gas station and Lincoln elementary school. Lincoln was one of those schools that look like a school should look, three story white brick with huge double hung windows.

My mother, Ruth, and my father, Henry

My folks were the best. They gave me unconditional love and on my 16th birthday my dad bought me a used 1960 Volkswagen Beetle. It was a financial stretch for him, but he told me, "my dad bought me a car when I was 16 and you should have one too". It was a goal for him and I was in heaven. I bought a Whitney catalogue to see what chrome attachments I could add. My next-door neighbor, Ben, was three years younger than me, but he enthusiastically helped me spruce up my car. It was faded salmon colored with a soft sunroof. The only gauges on the dashboard were a speedometer and an odometer, no fuel gauge. If the car started to sputter from a lack of gas, the driver needed to reach down to the floor near the gas pedal and turn a lever that gave the car an extra gallon of gas that could be used to go to a gas station. That happened to me once in the middle of Pittsburgh's Liberty Tunnel, an experience that convinced me to keep the gas tank full.

At age 16, I was in High School and was able to drive the mile and a half to school from my house rather than walk. This also gave me a feeling of independence. On weekends, Ben and I would go for drives to explore and to see what we could see. There was just one problem. I looked very young. This resulted in my being stopped by the police for driving under age. The combination of my youthfulness and my friend being three years younger than me presented a picture to the police that was irresistible. It was so annoying. We would be driving along and next thing we knew we would see the flashing red lights in the rear view mirror. (Police lights were red at that time.) What would follow was, "Ok sonny, get out of the car you aren't old enough to drive". I would then explain that I am. This resulted in the typical, "show me your license" followed by disbelief and the assumption that the license was falsified. After much ado I would be allowed to continue.

Then, an idea came to Ben and me. Rather than being annoyed and interrupted we could actually turn this into a game that we called Cop Catching. The idea of the game was to drive into an area where we were not known to the local police (most of the police in our area now knew me), and we would look for squad cars. When we saw a likely candidate, we would drive up beside the car. When the cop looked over at me I would look at him then snap my head straight ahead and slow down. This combination of my appearance and guilty reaction would catch them every time. They would pull me over; go through the routine just described, and eventually let me go. Before they left, however, we would record their badge number in a little red book in my glove compartment. As I recall, we had documented over a hundred badge numbers before we ended our spree of cop catching.

Oddly, about ten years later I had a flashback of my cop catching days while I was commanding a U.S. Air Force airdrop in Germany. One weekend my airdrop crew and I rented a car and drove to Luxemburg to see the sights. I was the designated driver.

As I was driving through the city, I stopped at a traffic light. As I waited for the light to change, I heard a whistle and looking out my left window I saw a police officer running toward me loudly blowing his whistle. He approached the car shouting in several different languages. Finally he said something I understood, "Shut off your car". He asked me for my driver's license. I had both a NJ driver's license and an international drivers license from AAA. I had no idea what I had done wrong, but thought I must have violated one of the international signs on the road. After a long pregnant pause he said, "You look young to drive". I was an Air Force Captain and the senior officer of my crew. Imagine the peals of laughter I had to live through from my Lieutenant and sergeant after we drove away. Somehow, cop-catching at age 26 isn't as much fun as at age 16.

Trick Night: Ben and I had lots of fun together. We would go out the night before Halloween to see what innocent trouble we could get into. They called it "Trick Night" in Pittsburgh. The best prank we ever pulled was on our friends and neighbors the Barnes. I lived in the house on the corner of the block; Ben lived next to me, and the Barnes were two houses up the block from Ben.

Ben was actually more of a troublemaker than I was, but I added a sense of civility and moderation to his enthusiasm that made us a good combination. Ben loosened me up and I straightened him up. His parents would often lock Ben in his room as punishment for what they considered to be mischief. Our street was a tree-lined hill with brick single-family homes that were all built in the 40s. The houses were closely spaced, that had deep yards running halfway through the block. The architecture of each house was different. My room was on the third floor of our house and it was directly across from Ben's room on his second floor. One day, when his parents were out, Ben and I rigged up an intercom and a clothesline pulley between our rooms. In this way we could continue to communicate when he was in lock-up and I could send him over potato chips and soda to ease his stay.

My house is on the left, Ben's house on the right.
His bedroom is the lower window in the picture.

One year, Ben and I hatched a plan to hit the Barnes' for trick night. Tom senior was a great guy. He was a manufacturers representative who sold candy to candy stores. He would occasionally generously donate some of his candy samples to us to sell on the sidewalk in the summer. It was great. When other kids were selling lemonade, we were selling Milky Way bars. He had a heart of gold. He coached our little league team and was a scoutmaster. He was also an extrovert who did things with gusto. We would play basketball in their yard and when a basket was made you could hear it all over the neighborhood. So Ben and I knew that it would be a real event to see his reaction to a good trick.

Ben on the left, I'm on the right.

The plan worked flawlessly. All we needed was a screwdriver and a small wire with an alligator clip on each end. We waited until about 8 pm when it was dark. We crept up to the Barnes' house and could see through their glass front and storm doors that they were watching TV in the living room. They were facing opposite the door. Their house was a beige and orange brick two-story house with a front porch about two feet wider on each side of the door. Once we determined that the Barnes' were all concentrating on the TV we went around to the back door. The garage was detached so there were only two ways out of the house, the front glass door and the back door. Both doors had wooden storm doors with glass inserts. We quietly opened the back storm door and removed the door handle and the rod that went through the door with the other handle attached and laid them on the cement porch outside the door. When we closed the door it latched. There was no way to open the latched door without inserting something into the hole where the handle rod had been removed. We then went around to the front door. This was the tricky part. We quietly did the same thing to the front storm door as well, fortunately without them seeing us. This essentially locked them in their house.

Now to spring the trap: I unscrewed the doorbell button by the door and connected the two contact points with the alligator clip wire. This set the doorbell ringing continuously. Ben and I ran across the street to hide in the bushes to watch the fun. The result was incredible.

The Barnes' knew it was trick night so the first reaction was young Tom (who is my age) yanking open the interior door with a yell to catch the person pushing the button. But he saw no one. After some confusion, Tom senior came to the door and tried to go outside. That is when he discovered that the door handles were laying on the concrete in front of the door. He yelled to young Tom to go around back. This was followed by more yelps when they discovered that the back door was in the same condition. Of course all this time the doorbell was buzzing loudly. Things hit a feverish pitch as they tried to open the front door with a screwdriver. After many expletives and considerable scrambling their efforts eventually paid off and they were able to quickly disarm the buzzer and reassemble their doorknobs. It was quite a challenge to restrain our laughter and sneak away unnoticed. I suppose there was no doubt in the Barnes' minds who did it, however Ben and I counted this a 10 out of 10 for trick night success. We were also glad that Ben didn't go to lock-up or need the soda and chip lifeline as a result of our trick night actions.

If you think this was a bit immature, it was, but I was young and it was also a time of innocence. Of all the crazy things I did as a kid, my going in objective was that no one and no one's property would be hurt. Being destructive is not a challenge or the right thing to do.

Tom Barnes and his younger brother Fred

Boy Scouts: In spite of the trick night joke I just described, young Tom Barnes and I were good lifelong friends. We went to school together, went to the same church, and were in the Boy Scouts together. He took things a bit more seriously than I did, but we both enjoyed camping and being out in the woods. Tom became an Eagle Scout. I didn't, but I am sure that every Boy Scout has stories of a memorable camping trip. Here is mine.

On one camping trip our troop went to the Fort Necessity campground. We arrived Friday evening and set up our campsite, lit fires from wood that was provided by the park service, and cooked dinner. In the middle of the night it started to rain. Boy, did it rain. Tom and I were in the same army surplus waxed-cotton tent. We tried to sleep through the maelstrom outside and finally did fall asleep. About 4 AM I woke to see Tom floating out of the tent. I guess I was slightly up hill from Tom because I was still on the ground. The water was rushing so fast around and through our tent that his air mattress had begun to float and he was heading down stream. By then we were both awake and I was scrambling to pull him back into the tent.

Tom is third from the left and I am third from the right

When the sun came up we emerged to find the campground awash in mud. We all jumped to and split logs to make a boardwalk between the tents and somehow started a fire. We had to have things right, because all of our parents were to visit about lunchtime. Everyone wanted to impress his parents with what great scouts we were. My job was to stir the soup that was in a big kettle over the fire. When my parents arrived I was stirring with great gusto and they were proud to see me at work and the campground we had all made.

Suddenly there was a shout, "FIRE". I looked down and saw that I had been standing with the toes of my rubber boots in the fire and they had started to blaze. They were the old style rubber boots with the metal latches that held them tight around your pant legs over your shoes. My parents looked shocked as I began running around with my toes on fire. I doused them with water only to discover that the boots had burnt open and bonded to my shoes underneath. As a result, I was pouring water into my shoes soaking my feet. All I can say is that I certainly did impress my parents, and all the others as well, but not as I had hoped. I don't think that there is a burning shoe merit badge, but if so, I earned it that day.

Jim Brennan: One of my best friends growing up was Jim Brennan. Jim's family and mine would get together at each other's houses and at Jim's grandparents farm outside of Pittsburgh. The farm was a wonderful place with a big man-made lake where we would swim and chase frogs. Jim was my best man, and I was his, when we each were married.

When we were very young the kids in our neighborhood played a game of tag. Of course as kids do, one would tag the other and say, "you're it, I quit" leaving the other player no options. Jim and I decided that that wasn't fair so we agreed that the game should never be over…and it still isn't. From that time on whenever we get together the parting action is to reactivate the game leaving one of us "it" until our next time together. Here is a picture of the final scene at Jim's wedding many years later. (By the way Jim, if you are reading this, you are "it".)

City & Country: My great grandfather on my father's side came from Germany in 1869 at age 14. He started as a grocery clerk in NJ and eventually owned a department store in Hicksville, Long Island, NY. His store furnished the supplies to the Vanderbilt's, Roosevelt's, and other estates on the north shore of Long Island. My father moved to Pittsburgh to attend Carnegie Tech University where he met my mother. Her family were farmers. The result for me as a boy growing up, was a life that included all that the city and country had to offer.

City. My folks belonged to the University Club of Pittsburgh and went there Tuesday nights to bowl and Saturday nights for dinner and to dance. By the time I was about thirteen years old, they would occasionally take me and I would dance with my mother to the big band sounds. I had been prepared for this by attending Genevieve Jones dancing class when I was in junior high school. It was one of those awkward experiences where all the boys stood on one side of the room and the girls on the other until we were compelled to count off and go meet our partner. I will say, however, I did learn how to dance and got to dance with a girl even though I looked like I was 10 years old, which did not impress most girls at the time.

I had an important role to play when my parents took me to the club when I was in grade school. They would go to the cocktail lounge for a drink with their friends and I was stationed with Chirp the bartender. I was responsible for fruit. For example, someone would order an "old fashioned", Chirp would mix the drink, and I would install the slice of orange and cherry. I guess that was all right it being a private club, and it sure entertained me. I still like a cherry in my drink to this day.

For my Dad's vacation every summer we would visit my grandfather on Long Island and sometimes go into Manhattan. It was there that I developed my taste for seafood, the ocean, and perhaps women. My Grandfather's house was two blocks from the main street in Hicksville, Long Island. No, I am not making this up. Hicksville was named after the Hicks family and was certainly not a hick town. His house was on a block with two churches.

When I was about eight years old, I was playing in the back yard and I remember distinctly a little girl who came into the yard and we played games together. She told me that her mother was attending a meeting at the Church. After some time she had to go. Fast forward to 1971. I am a First Lieutenant in the Air Force and on an American Express alpine tour on vacation. The first stop on the tour was the castle in Heidelberg, Germany. They had a "meet the others on the tour" event in the wine cellar. I met a girl named Kathie in the wine cellar. We started talking and discovered that she was from Long Island. After further discussion she related a story to me of her mother going to a church meeting and her remembering playing with a little boy who was visiting for the summer. She is now my wife.

Country. On weekends and holidays we would often visit relatives. My grandmother was a chicken farmer. She had five acres with a beautiful grass meadow in front of her mission style stone farmhouse. Behind the house was the vegetable garden leading to the two buildings housing the chickens. The big building was for the chickens that were laying the eggs and a smaller building for the adolescent birds and what we called the peepers. The peepers were the fuzzy yellow newborns. They ran around a circular enclosure with a heat lamp over them to stay warm. As they got older and began to grow feathers, the enclosure would be opened and they would join the adolescents. The tricky part was when the adolescents were to be moved to the adult chicken coop. I was invited to assist during one of these moves. What an experience!

The move was scheduled after sunset. Chicken crates were pre-positioned outside the adolescent coop. We suited up. After all the chickens were asleep and all was quiet in the coop we made our move. Each of us had a crate and we began picking up the chickens and putting them into the crates. Then all hell broke loose. The chickens didn't like being awakened and they didn't want to go into the crates. Chickens squawking...feathers flying...family members darting to and fro in the near dark. It was unforgettable. Then we had to carry the chicken laden crates to the main coop. Well, the older chickens weren't happy to be woken up and have the new chickens in their territory so the whole fracas began again. This, of course, had to be repeated until all the chickens had been transferred. What the new chickens didn't know was how nice their new accommodations would be. The walls of the main coop and rows of shelves 5 feet high in the center of the building were covered with square boxes facing out into the room. Each box had fresh straw in the bottom. Each chicken had it's own box, and in the morning, after the eggs were collected, the doors were opened and the chickens would go out into the chicken yard to eat and mingle. It was amazing to me that chickens need to eat stones as well as corn to grind up the corn in their gullet.

My grandmother sold eggs and chicken potpies. I didn't like to watch the potpie process, but the eggs were another matter. Each morning she would take the eggs to the cellar to the candling machine. She would load the eggs into a big hopper then sit in front of the machine. There was a trough from the hopper down to a viewing station with a bright light shining through the egg to the viewer. She would look at each egg to make sure that there were no chicken embryo's present and then step on a foot peddle. The next egg would then roll into view. She would then sort them for size and box them for sale. People would drive up the long entry drive all day long and come to the house to buy eggs and potpies.

My Aunt Net and Uncle Lyle lived on another farm about 30 miles away. Uncle Lyle raised cattle and Christmas trees, but was primarily the head of maintenance for a coalmine near where they lived. He was a Swede and a mountain of a man with a heart of gold. He was the kind of guy who repaired and reconfigured his own farm equipment and bulldozer. Walking into his barn was like stepping into a machine shop. He loved nature and he loved to hunt. When deer season opened he would go to his camp in the mountains. He would fill three freezers with venison and that is what his family would live on all year long. He was also a good taxidermist. There were deer heads over the fireplace, a pheasant or two here and there, and other assorted animals around the house. My first memories of their house are that it was cozy and warm with a big fireplace, no TV, and a party line phone on the wall. You only picked up the phone receiver when you heard two short rings and one long one. Many years later when my wife, Kathie, was there, he asked her to get something out of the freezer. She was surprised to discover that it was a huge frozen white owl that was waiting for his next taxidermy effort. He laughed, but she was not so amused.

Unfortunately Uncle Lyle did not live to see his granddaughter get married, but he was there in spirit. He had put away a shotgun for her years before as a gift for her wedding day because he knew that she also loved to hunt and shoot. After the ceremony, all the wedding party took turns shooting the gun in the air as a memorial to him and celebration for her.

My Uncle Harold also had a farm. He was my father's brother. After my Grandfather died and the department store was sold, Harold sold his farm on Long Island to a developer and bought a 100-acre farm near Gettysburg, PA. It was a beautiful place. The restored red brick 1700s farmhouse had an old wooden school building attached. It still had its bell. The barn was several stories high with stalls for cattle underneath and hay and farm equipment above. There was also a calf barn, pigpen, chicken coop, equipment building, and a tenant house. Harold raised cattle and had a couple of horses among other animals. Tennessee Walking Horses were his favorites. He had horse drawn buggies that he had restored that we could ride. As an only child, I enjoyed being with my cousins, Russ, Dan, and Jim, and feeling part of a big family. As kids, we used to like to go to the Gettysburg Battlefield and play Civil War soldiers. We would hide in Devil's Den, a rocky part of the battlefield with caves and outcroppings. It was there that we would plan our attack on imaginary armies.

Uncle Harold and cousin Jim in front of their house
Note bell on schoolhouse.

One day we went to a local town fair near Harold's farm. We were having great fun trying our luck at the various games of skill when we heard a large commotion. People were muttering and pointing, and there he was, President Eisenhower! Eisenhower's farm was nearby and he had stopped by to see the fair and greet the people there. No fanfare, no speeches, just the President walking around talking to people. My father came up to me to ensure that I realized the magnitude of this event. As we were talking, we noticed that people were still shooting at the shooting gallery. This seemed very surprising because the shooters were using real rifles shooting 22 shorts at metal targets that marched across the gallery and which spun when you hit them. We couldn't believe that they would let the shooting continue while the President was there. We got our answer. When the President left so did the people at the shooting gallery. All the shooters were secret service agents. Presidential security certainly has changed a lot since those days.

In looking back, I realize how blessed I was as a child to know the joys of both the City and the Country in such an intimate way while living in the suburbs.

Mt. Lebanon High School: So there I was in the cafeteria lunch line at the beginning of 10th grade when a teacher with a white streak in his black hair came up to me and asked me to talk to him. We sat and he asked me if I had considered joining the wrestling team. It turned out that he was George Lamprinakos, the school wrestling coach.

Not being much of a fighter, I told Coach Lamp, as we called him, that I hadn't. He told me that he wanted to recruit me for the 88-pound weight class. There were no boys in the school that weighed that little so I was it. If I accepted, I would get a varsity letter in my first year in high school, become part of a great team, and receive recognition from my school and my parents. I accepted. What followed were workouts every day after school and efforts by coach and teammates to turn me into a wrestler.

For me, wrestling started back at the cafeteria where the school paid for me to have milkshakes and desserts at lunch to fatten me up. I only weighed 75 pounds and I would be wrestling opponents who were struggling to get down to 88, a 15% weight advantage. Learning the basic moves was easy for me, but implementing them was a different story. There was no one near my weight with whom I could practice with in preparation for my first match. I had never been to a wrestling match before. As it turned out matches started with the lightest weight class, so I was first up at my very first match. My opponent and I came out onto the mat and faced each other at a circle in the center of the mat. He was a black kid from Westinghouse High School near the steel mills. His arms were as big as my legs. I stared from him to the referee to my parents sitting in the bleachers to my coach and then I heard the whistle. We lunged toward each other and I spun to get out of my opponents way. We then circled each other and he went for my legs. Bam, my face hit the mat. I turned to try a maneuver called a switch, but he kept slamming me forward. The ref had held up two fingers indicating that he had earned two points for the takedown. The rest of the match is a blur to me now, but to make a long story short, he won. The good news is that I did not get pinned and our team didn't lose as much as it would have if I had not been on the team.

Other members of the team were great athletes like Drew Bachman who went on to win state championships. Several times I would win because the other team couldn't find anyone as small as me so I would win by default, but on the whole my wrestling career was not stellar. What was stellar was being on the team. It was physically, mentally, and emotionally tough, but it taught me valuable lessons that came in handy later in life as I faced Air Force pilot training and the war in Vietnam. I look back at my coach and teammates with great love and affection for what they did for me. I would have never experienced being on an athletic team if it were not for Coach Lamp pulling me out of the cafeteria line.

Wrestling was not my only avocation in high school. One of the many activities I was involved with was stage crew. Our school was fortunate to have a stage that could host professional theatre as well as school productions. Mr. Ramsay was my off-the-mat coach teaching me the art of stage productions from lighting to set design and curtain pulling. I worked my way up the seniority list to the point where I was running the spotlight from my own little room in the back of the auditorium. We had a carbon arc spotlight. The light was created when two carbon rods about the thickness of a pencil came together. That created a spark of light as bright as a welder's arc behind lenses that magnified and focused the light on the subject on the other side of the auditorium. I would mount the rods and turn the crank until they touched. When the spark ignited I would back them apart slightly and turn on the motor. The motor would feed the rods continuously within a 1/16 of an inch from each other creating a continuous arc light. I could look into the lamp from the side through a green lens to adjust the spacing if necessary. The most memorable time was when I spotlighted Helen Hayes. She came to perform and I was able to work with professionals from the union.

While working on stage crew I met Bruce Chriswell. He was on the sound squad and a year behind me in school. We hit it off and became good friends. His sound squad duties became important to me personally on my graduation day. There were about 625 students in my graduating class. The graduation ceremony was to be held in the football stadium. The faculty decided that the most impressive way to hold the ceremony was for the class in full cap and gown to march from the school building down a long flight of stairs around the walkway and into the stadium. We were to be organized by height as we marched in, then wind through the seats and sit in alphabetical order, quite a logistical feat. The day of commencement we all lined up and guess who was in the front of the line. We were to march by twos with a male on one side and a female beside.

So there I was next to the shortest girl in the class at the front of the procession. I had never met my commencement partner until the practice session. It was the two of us then about 75 females until another male showed up in the line. One good thing was that my parents didn't need to struggle to find me in line. The other good news was that I was able to get a movie of the grand event. As it turned out my friend Bruce was responsible running the sound system for the commencement. He was hiding in the ferns in front of the platform where the Principal was handing out the diplomas. I provided him with a 8mm movie camera and he filmed the entire event capturing my participation. It really pays to know the people working events.

Autobiography - And Other Funny Stories

Graduation

My time in high school was a wonderful phase of my life with two exceptions. The first was being in physics class when my teacher announced that President Kennedy had been shot. I am sure that if you were alive when this tragic event occurred you remember where you were. I was in Mr. Ruth's physics class. The second exception was my grades. Not up to my ability as they told me, a perfect 2.0. Fortunately, all ended up well in two respects. The first is that I got into the perfect college for me, the University of Akron. The second was a bolt from the blue. Thirty-five years after I graduated from Mt. Lebanon High School, my childhood friend, Tom Barnes, was a reporter for the Pittsburgh Post Gazette. Tom saw what I was doing at NASA in a note in my Christmas card and thought my career might be an interesting "local boy makes good" story. It was the same Tom Barnes whose house Ben and I played the prank on so many years before. Obviously he didn't hold that against me. Tom sent a photographer and a reporter to interview me. The story was published in an almost full-page article on page two of the Pittsburgh Post Gazette. The High School picked up on the Mt. Lebanon connection in the article. They invited me back to school to give the keynote presentation before the Cum Laude Society-- the society for high school scholars. You need a perfect 4.0 average to get into the society.

There I was, dressed in Harvard Master's Degree robes that I had earned twenty years after graduating from high school, speaking of the adventures of my life and challenging the students who were being inducted into the society to grab life and be adventurous. They presented me with an honorary membership in the society. What an unexpected thrill. As I said in my interview with the reporter, "I got Cs in high school, Bs in college, and A's at Harvard. Mt. Lebanon must be one tough school".

Pipe Grinding: After graduation from High School, I had a summer free prior to going to college. My father was the Vice President of Operations for the National Valve Manufacturing Company. That summer, and for the next two, I was allowed by the union to work as a laborer in one of my father's plants. They didn't make valves. Instead they made piping for power plants. In power plants there is the need for an extensive array of custom made pipes that carry the hot and cold gas and liquids around the plant.

In 1964 National Valve was involved in providing piping for nuclear power plants. They required pipes that would withstand very high temperatures and pressures. Some of these were steel pipes that had wall thicknesses of up to ten inches. The pipes would be heated and bent into a shape required by the engineering drawings and then welded to strait lengths. Because of all the safety requirements for nuclear power plants, each weld had to be without flaws. To determine this, a nuclear engineer would tape film around the weld on the outside of the pipe and thread a nuclear isotope into the pipe to take a picture of the weld somewhat like the dentist takes an x-ray of your teeth. If a flaw was detected the pipes would be ground down or cut apart and re-welded at great expense. To prepare for this process the welds had to be ground smooth both inside and out. The outside was a piece of cake. The inside was another story. Inside required a person to crawl inside the pipe to grind the weld. Guess who got that job? Yes, as the smallest guy around the job fell to me. It is quite a memorable experience.

I would suit up in a work suit like a flight suit with mask and gloves. One of the other guys would then lift me into the pipe and hand me a pneumatic grinder attached to a hose that supplied air pressure to operate the grinder. I would hold the grinder out in front of me as I inched into a pipe that was not much wider than me. Behind me they would shine a bright light and secure a huge fan to blow air from my feet toward my face. I would inch my way forward toward the weld like a worm until the grinding wheel was in line with the weld. I'd then hit the switch. The grinder would whir into action. I could feel its torque in my outstretched arms. Sparks would fly…and smoke would shoot ahead of me… blown by the giant fan. When my arms became too tired to grind any more they would pull me out by pulling on the grinder's hose. When the weld seemed smooth to me, they would give me some die to put on the weld that showed any imperfections that I had missed and I would go at it again. It was a heck of a summer job, but I was delighted to get the $3.75 an hour, big money at the time.

It was a great experience working with the laborers and supervisors at the plant. It was the perfect experience for a guy going to the University of Akron to study engineering and industrial management.

Chapter 2: Akron

Much to my dismay at the time, I did not get good enough grades in high school to go to my father's alma matter, Carnegie Tech in Pittsburgh, but I wanted to follow in my father's footsteps and become an engineer. The University of Akron was the perfect school for me. It was not too far from Pittsburgh, where I grew up, and it had an excellent engineering school featuring a co-op program after the first two years so that I could get both an education and practical experience. It has grown to be an incredible Ohio State University, but at the time it was mostly a local University with few out of town students. I made the most important career decision in my life before I had even taken one class.

There I was sitting in the admissions director's office with my parents going over the courses that I would take my freshman year. As an engineering student, there were not many choices, but one was all I needed. At the end of outlining the compulsory courses, the admissions director looked at me and said the following: "This is a land-grant university. You must take ROTC for the first two years. Do you want Army or Air Force?" Without a moment's hesitation or thought, I said, "I'd rather fly than walk". That decision, to go into Air Force ROTC, set the course for my entire professional career. Two years later as the Viet Nam war was building, my ROTC instructor said, "You need to make a choice. Do you want to go advanced and become an officer, or drop out of ROTC and be drafted?" I decided to go advanced. He then said, "Well now that you will become an Air Force officer would you like to become a pilot or something else?" Well, something else didn't sound so great, and the rest is history.

Zippy: I guess I have a knack for being recruited in cafeterias, but it happened again in College. One morning while eating in the dorm cafeteria the director of student services approached me and asked if I would come talk to him. His name was Dudley Johnson. He told me that the school was looking for a new school mascot and asked me if I would be interested. I asked him what the mascot was. He told me that it was a kangaroo. I asked him why I would want to be a kangaroo? He said that I would get a ride and free tickets to all the games, have a great view from my seat on the sidelines, and I'd get to hang out with the cheerleaders. Hanging out with he cheerleaders made the case for me, and I became the first University of Akron mascot named Zippy.

Being Zippy gave me notoriety around campus and many interesting experiences, but none as memorable as my performance on the basketball court. The University of Akron had a wonderful basketball team including a center, Bill Turner who was 6'8" tall. For a typical basketball game, the cheerleaders would go through their routines and I would horse around, dribble my painted ball, and take a shot or two. This was not as easy as it sounds because I had to do this while wearing a giant paper-mache kangaroo head with two slits above the nose to look out. As I was preparing for an upcoming game, I got the idea that it would be great if I could dunk the ball like Bill was able to do. I thought that this would bring the crowd to their feet and be a great accomplishment especially since I was so short.

As the players came onto the court for some practice before the game, I spoke to Bill and asked him if he would help me with this idea. I asked him if he would stand under the net and lift me up so that I could dunk the ball. The idea was that I would dribble the ball toward the basket and as I approached he would lift me up and I would dunk the ball. He agreed and we set the plan in motion. Unfortunately we did not practice this maneuver. As we got closer to game time, he went under the basket and I made some gestures to get the crowd's attention. Then I dribbled the ball toward the basket, he grabbed me by the thighs and lifted me up. I reached forward to put the ball in the basket, and then it happened. As I reached forward my nose hit the rim of the basket lifting my kangaroo head. Now I was blind because the sight holes were aimed straight up and I couldn't see the basket. I ended up falling forward and grabbed the rim of the basket to steady myself. With that, Bill stepped away and I was left hanging from the basket. That did bring the crowd to their feet, but not as I had intended. With that, the referee came running toward me blowing his whistle. As he came beneath me he shouted for me to let go. Well, I was not about to do that being so far in the air and not able to see. He then shouted that if I bent the rim he would have to cancel the game. This was in the old days when the rims were firmly mounted to the backboard. He continued shouting and blowing his whistle until I felt some friendly hands on my feet. The team had surrounded me and caught me as I fell.

I am not sure if this was the high point or low point of my mascot career, but it was very gratifying that the team came to my rescue and the school did not suspend me. I never tried anything like that again. It also taught me a valuable lesson, before attempting anything new and risky, simulate and practice.

TKE Fraternity: The second half of my freshman year was the time to pledge a fraternity. The Greek system was big at Akron U and the focus of almost all of campus social life. I pledged Tau Kappa Epsilon fraternity. I pledged TKE because of the great mix of guys and a wonderful Victorian mansion that was the TKE house. In 1965, when I pledged, life was simpler and more innocent than in later years. Fraternities would serenade sororities and compete in events like Songfest where teams from each fraternity would be judged for their singing performance and awarded trophies. Pledges would have house clean-up duties and would be mentored by the more senior members of the fraternity. That was particularly important for me. As an only child it was great to have Bob Nettles as my big brother. I had never experienced living with people my own age before. Having fraternity brothers who were two years ahead of me and willing to mentor me also helped with my engineering studies. And then there were parties.

I still looked pretty young in those days so getting a date was a bit of a challenge. The fraternity was the answer. Friday night was fraternity night when we would all go out to a local disco type place and dance. You could drink 3.2 beer at 18 in Ohio and the discos had live bands. In the group you could easily meet people and have some fun. Saturday night was date night so if you were able to meet someone on Friday you could ask her out on Saturday. There were also mixers between fraternities and sororities.

The major event of the school year was in May when a fraternity and sorority would join in making a May Day float for the big parade down Main Street in Akron. The engineers in the fraternity would design and create the structure for a float that would be built on a flat bed trailer. The structure would be covered with chicken wire and filled with fluffies. Fluffies were made of crinkled up crepe paper about 6 inches long with a wire twisted around the middle. The crepe paper was then pulled to create something that resembled a flower and wired into the chicken wire to make the float panels. It took thousands of fluffies to make a float. We spent a month or two in the evenings making these flowers with the sorority that our fraternity was paired with that year. Creating the float was a great way to talk to and really get know the members of the sorority. The after parade-party was always a highpoint of the year.

After a semester of study, pledging, and Zippy, it was now the end of my freshman year and time for hell week. This was the week after school ended and the time that would make or break me in terms of joining the fraternity. For my pledge class of about 25 guys, it was a time when we had to move into the loft above the garage and follow the direction of our pledge trainer, the Hegamon. Most of the time we were working on the house, painting, cleaning etc. However there were also times of harassment and humiliation. There was a pledge book that described the history of the fraternity and we were told that we needed to memorize all the important details because we would have to pass the Prytanis (President's) Quiz as the last act of hell week. One wrong answer would mean expulsion from the fraternity. So for a week we worked, did pushups, ran around like idiots at all hours of the day and night, and studied.

Finally, the Prytanis Quiz night was here. Exhausted and anxious, our Big Brothers would take us into a room where we were alone and blindfolded waiting to be called. I stared into the darkness of my blindfold trying to remember the names of the 5 TKE founders, significant dates, etc. Then the moment was here.

I was led up the stairs to the third floor chapter room. I heard the knock on the door, the Prytanis said come in, and the rustling of the chapter members as I arrived. I was handed a strap with a weight on it to hold outright and the quiz began. There were to be three questions. The first two were fairly easy then came the third. I couldn't recall the answer...I asked if he would repeat it...my head started to spin and my arm holding the weight started to drop. After all this work and all the people that I became close to over the last year, how could I not have the answer to this question? I stammered and admitted that I didn't know. Immediately the weight was yanked from my hand and I was ejected from the room. My Big Brother led me back down to the room I had been in before. I was upset and he tried to comfort me. He asked me why I hadn't known the answer and I tried to explain all that I had done to get the answers right. He told me that he had really wanted me in the fraternity and that he would go back up to the chapter room and try to convince the active members to give me another chance. Then I was left alone. The rest of this ceremony is a secret of the fraternity, but let's just say that I made it. The actives started clapping and I finally understood that this last challenge was to test my desire to be a member and that I had passed. We all started to hug and congratulate each other and the party began. I still get emotional as I think back on the ceremony. It taught me the lesson that things aren't always what they seem and that perseverance is the key to achieving something important.

Engineering: At the end of my sophomore year I had begun to realize that engineering wasn't the career for me. Between studies, being Zippy, and fraternity activities my grades were in the Cs and heading south. I knew it was time to switch majors. My Big Brother suggested that I transfer to Industrial Management. To show you how naive I was at the time, I responded that my family didn't own a business (because several of my family friends families did) so why would I move to that major? He told me that companies hire people with business degrees and in fact the business degree people often hire engineers. With that revelation, I transferred to Industrial Management and my academic career started to be successful.

If we fast-forward 33 years, I am working as the Senior Policy Advisor for Aviation at the National Science and Technology Council at the White House. I was asked to give a dinner speech at an AIAA International Lighter-Than-Air Symposium in Akron, Ohio. Akron is the home of lighter-than-air technology in America and still has a dirigible hanger. Lockheed Martin does research in the field there.

When the symposium organizers discovered from my biography that I had graduated from the University of Akron, they contacted the school and the press. As I arrived at the symposium, I was met by the current Zippy and several photographers who captured the moment of the original Zippy returning to Akron from the White House. It was an incredible moment. At the dinner, I was seated next to the President of the University, Luis Proenza. As part of the festivities, he presented me with a gold Zippy lapel pin and I presented him with a letter sweater that I wore as Zippy all those years before.

Presenting my ZIPPY sweater to
Akron President Luis Proenza and Zippy

After dinner, he and I retired to the lounge and were joined by the Director of the Lockheed Martin plant in Akron where they were working on the next generation of lighter-than-air vehicles. As we talked, I asked Luis why the University of Akron had such a great engineering program, but no degree in aeronautical engineering? This would be particularly appropriate because Akron was the birthplace of lighter-than-air in America. To shorten a long story, the University subsequently hired a new engineering dean, George Haritos and after discussions over two years, he created an aeronautical engineering program that is unique in the nation. The unbelievable thing for me is that after not being able to be successful in engineering, I had facilitated the creation of an aerospace engineering program at my alma mater.

At the end of my Zippy days, I was driving to Evansville, Indiana for the regional basketball finals with three of my fraternity brothers. I had a red Opel Kadett. It was winter and it began to snow. As I drove down the super highway I hit a patch of ice and the car started to slide sideways. Then I hit a dry patch and the car started to spin. We went into the snow covered grass median strip then up on the opposite side of the divided highway then back into the median, then up then down, and finally came to rest on the pavement. As our hearts stopped pounding and we had regained our composure we were delighted to see that the car had not rolled over and that we were all just fine. The only problem was that we didn't know what side of the road we were on or in what direction we needed to head. We had to retrace our marks in the snow to see where we had left the highway in-order to proceed.

Then, one of the guys told me that he knew a short cut, so we exited the highway and proceeded down a secondary road. The road got narrower and narrower as we proceeded into the woods. As we rounded a bend we were shocked to discover a huge fence with guard towers, search lights, dogs and sentries at the dead end of the road. I think the guards were as shocked as we were. It turned out to be a Naval Weapons Depot in the middle of Indiana. Why was the Navy in the middle of the woods, hundreds of miles from the nearest naval base? Your guess is as good as mine. We eventually made it to Evansville, but it was quite an adventure getting there.

Yearbook: In 1967 I was a junior and a fraternity brother came to me and told me that the school was looking for an editor of the college yearbook the <u>Telbook</u>. At Akron U every student received a yearbook as part of his or her student fees so the challenge was to create a book that captured the year for everyone. Up to this point yearbooks had sections like seniors, sports teams, fraternities, clubs, etc. As I interviewed for the position, I suggested that we might try a different approach by integrating these shots into a book that was chronologically based starting with the first day of school that year and ending with graduation and the seniors. To my great joy and surprise, I got the job, Editor-in-Chief.

Over the summer, between my junior and senior year, I was besieged with offers from printing companies and companies who wanted to take senior pictures. To my surprise, some offered me sizable kickbacks. They were removed from consideration, but taught me what to be cautious of while serving as a financial decision maker. Having decided on the companies I would work with, my next goal was to pick a staff and move into my office in the student center.

The University had a professional photographer that I was to use, Bob Wilkey. He was fabulous. Fantastic artistic shots of campus, basketball players in flight by the basket, campus organizations in unique settings, candid shots of students and faculty when they least expected it, all came flowing into the office from Bob's camera for us to arrange and add cryptic notes.

It was an incredible artistic opportunity and fun working with a talented staff. Finally the day came when boxes of thousands of books arrived for distribution, and I presented the first copy to my faculty advisor, Bob Sartoris. In my presence, he leafed through the book with smiles and complements until he got to one page. His mouth dropped open, he stared, and then a look of terror crossed his face. The page with the layout of the University Board-of-Trustees had the names transposed on the pictures. The Board-of-Trustees were mislabeled. The books could not be distributed with this mistake.

What could we do? After calls to the publisher and a lot of hand ringing, a solution was found. Reprint the offending page with a glue line on the edge and cut the page from every book with a razor and glue in the corrected page. Numerous people had reviewed the galley proofs, but the mistake had been overlooked.

The school loved the yearbook even if distribution was delayed by a week of cutting and pasting. I don't think anyone realized that there had been a mistake except our staff, who all manned the glue line. We all learned that attention to detail is very important.

ROTC: In the summer of my senior year I had to attend ROTC summer camp. For me, that consisted of driving to Dover Air Force Base in Delaware and getting my assignment to F Squadron. Our Squadron Commander was an AF navigator Roxy Stottler. We were housed in some vacant quarters on the base and taught discipline by having our shoes, underwear, bedding, etc in prescribed alignment like army boot camp. We had training classes, learned how to march, and did physical exercises. If we had anything out of line we got demerits and had to walk them off around the parking lot on weekends -- so we could not depart the base until all was completed.

In one exercise we had a certain time to finish a number of laps around the parade field or the entire team got demerits. As the shortest guy in the squadron, I had a hard time keeping up with the taller guys as we ran the laps. We were required to all finish together so the pressure was on. Some of the guys who were the best runners ran beside me to urge me on. We were a good team and learned that we all have different skills and detriments. The way to succeed is to help one another. This became clear when we had our survival training.

Charles H. Huettner

ROTC survival training wasn't anything like the real thing that I experienced after pilot training. It was more like a Boy Scout experience. All the squadrons were taken to a wooded area and taught how to make a fire, pitch a tent, etc. The one incredible exception was the exercise in killing a chicken. Yes, killing a chicken.

The idea was that if you are to survive in the woods you would need to somehow trap something to eat. This was simulated with a live chicken. The instructors thought it would be funny if they picked the least likely person from each squadron and had them dispatch the chicken in front of the other squadron members. This was a bit sadistic because several of the selectees were from inner city Brooklyn and had never seen a live chicken before. There was a small ditch that ran through the campsite so the unlucky selectee from the various squadrons was put on one side of the ditch and handed a chicken. Everyone else stood on the other side of the ditch to learn the lesson. Picture about eight guys holding live chickens by the neck. The Commander instructed these guys that the way to kill their chicken was to hold the chicken by the head and snap the neck killing the chicken. Of course the chicken doesn't stop flapping for some time after the deed is done, but they should just hold on and all would settle down.

So at the command the eight guys started snapping their chickens. Of course the chickens started flapping and squawking. Since snapping didn't seem to be working for some of the selectees they started beating their chickens on the ground. This resulted in an uproar from the audience. One selectee decided that he would start swinging his chicken around and around in a circle over his head. This was one of those times that confirmed for me that there is a God in heaven. On about the tenth swing of the chicken it must have given up the ghost. If not the ghost then at lease all that was in it's bowel. A steady stream of chicken shit flew out of the chicken and hit the Commander in the face. That ended the demonstration.

As my college days came to a close it was time to prepare to enter the U.S. Air Force. During my senior year, I was very fortunate to be put into the ROTC flight program that paid for me to earn my private pilot's license at Freedom Field a small general aviation airport near Akron. It was a thrill for me to get my pilot's license while still in school. I took my friends for flights around Ohio and even to Kelly Island where it was only possible to go by boat or air. I even took our yearbook photographer for a flight over the school so that he could take pictures from the air. I earned my pilots license and was about to complete my academic courses for my degree so I was all set to get my Air Force Commission at graduation. There was only one more hurdle and that was significant. I had to pass my Air Force flight physical.

I knew that I was in good health, and my eyesight was 20/20 so what could be the problem? My great fear was the scale with the height rod. The minimum height for Air Force pilot training was 5' 4" and I was just shy of that at that time. I know that sounds crazy, but the height limit was the challenge for me. I had always looked young and been small, but now this was serious. My ROTC instructor would detail me to the gym to hang on the high bar to stretch after class. For weeks before the physical I did all I could to be taller. Finally the fateful day came.

I sat in the waiting room to keep as much weight as possible off my back. I knew that that was the key to my success. Then the nurse called me into the exam room. She had me sit on the table and began to take my blood pressure. As I sat there I saw the dreaded scales and height rod. I knew that this was it. While she was pumping up the pressure cuff she asked me how much I weighed. I told her. Then she asked me how tall I was? I couldn't believe it. I told her 5'4". She wrote it down. I was thrilled. I knew that I had passed. What joy!!!... Until she said, "I'm sorry, you have a problem... You have high blood pressure. We can't accept you." AHHH!! I pleaded with her to give me another chance. I told her that I was nervous about the exam and asked if I could rest a minute. She consented and I passed on the second attempt. I was to become an Air Force officer and go to pilot training.

Chapter 3: UASF

Laredo Air Force Base Texas

I was commissioned a second lieutenant my last day of school and headed home then west to Laredo, Texas. It was March 31, 1969 when I reported for duty at Laredo Air Force Base after driving across country from my home in Pittsburgh. I checked into the Bachelor Officers Quarters and found myself in a room in a 1940s building sharing a bath with the guy in the room next door. The good news was that my quarters were next door to the Officers Club where we ate our meals and spent our recreation time. What I quickly discovered was that there were only three English-speaking girls of my age in the entire city of Laredo, the Guerra sisters. I spoke to one of them on the second week of my stay and was told there was a six-month waiting list if I wanted to go out with her. Laredo AFB had the reputation of being the closest thing to a foreign assignment on US soil, only a mile or two by air to Mexico. My classmate, great friend, and adopted brother, Ken Alm, and I spent 33 weekends traveling the 125 miles from Laredo to either Corpus Christie or San Antonio to escape the pressures of pilot training and have some fun.

It was exciting to be in pilot training. Our class of about 60 was split into two sections. I was in 70-06B so named for the year we were scheduled to graduate. We had academics in the morning and flew in the afternoon while the 06A section did the reverse. We changed mornings and afternoon flying with the other section weekly. The first day we saw a framed board with our AF pilot's wings above our name and were told that only half of us would probably make it. As time went on, more and more names and wings were pulled from the board, keeping the pressure on us all to do our very best.

The yearlong program involved academics including weather, flight planning, navigation, flight regulations and procedures, and aircraft systems. We also got to parasail and jump off towers to practice a technique called a parachute landing fall.

Actual flying started in a Cessna 172 labeled a T-41 by the Air Force. This was to separate out the guys who got airsick and wouldn't follow instructions. We then moved into the T-37 side-by-side jet trainer called the "Tweet" because of the high-pitched noise that its engines made. We all looked longingly for the day when we would get to move into the T-38, a white supersonic jet.

T-37 training flights were conducted at a remote airfield used only for training called Barfly. Barfly was a runway and a mobile control tower where students and instructors would watch each plane on final approach to see that there was a red light in the nose of the plane to indicate that the landing gear was in fact down and locked. If so, the pilot was cleared for a touch and go, if not a go around.

Perhaps I didn't mention that Laredo is in the middle of what is practically a desert. The tallest trees are actually bushes about 8 feet high and the ground is covered with leaf cactus. The weather report on the radio each morning was sunny and hot, highs near 100, today through November. It did rain twice while I was there and hailed once making my car look like someone had taken a ball peen hammer to it.

Barfly was in the middle of the cactus.

It was a real challenge to go to Barfly to control the landings. The challenge was not the job, but getting in and out of the mini-tower. It would routinely get to be 100 degrees during the day when we would be in this tower. The good news was that it was air-conditioned. The bad news was that the building would drip from condensation and that attracted wild life. The most onerous were brown recluse spiders. These spiders were about the size of dimes but there were thousands of them crawling all over the tower, and they were poisonous. To get into the tower you had to brush them away from the latch and key hole, unlock the door, then yank it open with as much force as possible to throw those who were in the cracks of the door to the ground, then jump in and slam the door. The process was repeated on exiting.

Barfly

T-37: The T-37 was a two pilot side-by-side jet trainer that the Air Force used to turn students into real pilots. We initially learned to navigate by looking out the cockpit window, not on instruments. For perhaps an obvious reason this is called dead-reckoning because you could die if you got lost. Later we were taught to navigate by using cockpit instruments. The instrument procedures would allow us to fly in low visibility and under air traffic control. We also learned safety maneuvers in case we had problems while flying.

One emergency maneuver procedure was a stall-spin recovery. I was blessed with one of the best pilots that I have ever known as my instructor, Glenn Prophet. He was a flight examiner and I was his only student. On my first try at this maneuver, Glenn took me out to a training area and went over the procedure.

First you put the plane into a stall by pulling back on the stick until the nose of the plane was pitched high and the power is pulled back. Eventually the plane begins to shutter and the stick shakes indicating a stall warning. Recovery from a stall is to lower the nose and add power, but for this maneuver the instructor would kick the rudder. That would put the plane into a spin. The plane now spins uncontrollably and falls toward the ground. The corrective action for this is to "abruptly pull the stick back and hold… rudder and ailerons neutral… abruptly bang the stick full forward and recover from the ensuing dive. Pulling the stick back ensures that you are not upside down and banging the stick forward breaks the stall so you can recover from this harrowing maneuver. I only made one mistake.

I had memorized the procedure so well that I rushed the steps. Unfortunately my instructor, Glenn, was tall. When I got into the cockpit I would raise my seat to the highest position he to the lowest. As I went though the procedure, I didn't realize that I had been successful on the first try so I tried it again. When I slammed the stick forward the second time we pulled a ton of negative Gs. What this means is that we were both launched forcefully upward in the cockpit. I heard this cracking sound as I worked to level the aircraft. I had been violently thrown against my shoulder straps, but was OK. I could not say the same for Glenn. As I looked over at him I could see that he had hit his head on the top of the canopy and his flight helmet had cracked, split in half, and fell to his left and right. I said, "I guess this means we are going back to base?" All he could do is shake his head. I didn't pass the maneuver that time around.

Finally I was checked out to go solo in the T-37 for my first cross-country flight. This flight was designed to let us apply our knowledge of flight planning, instrument flying, and going to a destination alone in the cockpit. I was heading to Barksdale AFB, Louisiana from Laredo Texas to spend the night.

As I walked to the aircraft that evening I was excited.

I had done all my flight planning and climbed into the cockpit confidently. It was afternoon when I started the engines and taxied out for takeoff behind a line of other students from my section. I received my clearance and took off on the flight, climbing to altitude heading to Barksdale. My flight plan had me going to an initial approach fix for an approach to runway 15 north of the field. When I got in range of the airport I contacted Barksdale approach control. They didn't answer. I tried again a short time later and there was still no answer. I could hear the other aircraft in my group talking to ATC, but they would not answer me. I recycled my radio, double checked the approach frequency, and made another call. My transmitter was not working.

We trained for radio-out procedures, so I thought I would simply follow the procedure and continue to my initial approach fix then descend on my scheduled time of arrival. As I continued to the approach fix, I heard the controllers say that the winds had changed and they were changing the runway direction to landing north runway 33. That meant that I would be landing opposite to the direction of all the other aircraft if I continued to follow my flight plan. What to do.... follow the procedures was what I was supposed to do, but that would not work.

About that time ATC discovered that I was not talking to them and they began to call me. I was not able to answer them. Finally they told me to go to the approach point for runway 33 and make my approach, so I turned and headed in the opposite direction. About then I realized that I was running low on fuel. My maneuvering to the second runway at low altitude was eating up my reserve.

I was caught between procedures that I was instructed to follow as a student and a real world crisis of simply landing as soon as possible. I chose the latter. I turned straight for the end of the landing runway and the controllers saw on their radar what I was doing. They cleared the way for me and I landed safely. As I taxied and turned to the parking spot my right engine flamed out for lack of fuel. I learned that day that there is a time to follow the rules and a time to do what needs to be done.

Formation flying: The next step in my training was to learn formation flying. It is a surreal experience. The idea is to line up behind your lead aircraft at an angle that puts the lead's wingtip in the star on the side of his plane. Once in position you were to slowly move forward along that line until you are within feet of the lead - like you see the Thunderbirds do at air-shows. Instructors can explain this to you on the ground, but the only way to really learn to do this is in the aircraft.

To begin, the instructor sitting next to you puts the plane in the formation position then says, "You got it" and lets go of the stick. What happens next is really messy. As I took the stick the aircraft started gyrating and pitching up and down as the lead sped away from me. The instructor took control and smoothly put the aircraft back into position. He said, "don't move the stick, just think the plane into position". After two more failed practice flights I was given one more chance to master formation flying. Then a miracle occurred. I did it. The instructor was right. Just think the plane into position and it goes there. Any conscious movement of the stick was too much. I passed formation flying and was able to move on to the T-38.

T37 Formation Flight

T-38: The T-38 is a beautiful plane; sleek, white, supersonic, afterburners, WOW. Long after pilot training I would say that they wasted the T-38 on inexperienced pilots. It was a joy to fly.

By now we were refining our flying skills and learning basic fighter maneuvers like close and extended trail. In close trail, the trailing aircraft positioned itself directly behind the lead aircraft and slightly below so that you were looking at the back end of the lead's jet engines. Lead would set 80% power so trail had 20% more power to play with. Then lead would try to lose the trailing aircraft. Climbing, diving, turning, the challenge was to stay "in". As you went upside down in turns you could only see lead. If you lost him, he was gone or you would run into him and be dead. Extended trail was similar, only both aircraft set the same power and maneuvered at a greater distance. This was like a dogfight in the movies. As lead would turn or climb you would try to move inside his turn to catch up to him. If you did it right, you could eventually form up on his wing and win the battle, all this at over 500 MPH. It was an unbelievable experience

T-38 Formation Flight (Note wing of my aircraft at lower left.).

Finally, the training was over and the time we had anticipated from the beginning was at hand. We were to get our assignments as Air Force Pilots. The process brought great anxiety. We were joined by the other section of our class and sat in a room with a blackboard in front. As we waited anxiously the Commander listed on the blackboard the aircraft that would be available for us to fly after pilot. This was at the height of the Viet Nam war so we knew that we were headed to war in whatever aircraft we were able to choose. When the list of aircraft was complete on the board the Commander read off the name of the student that had achieved the highest score in the class. He had the first pick from the list of aircraft on the board. Every examination and flight was graded and the score totals ranked the class members who finished successfully from top to bottom. My friend, Ken Alm, was number 2. He got a fighter. As each aircraft was chosen it would be erased from the board. I was number 20 on the list of about 60 that remained from both sections of our class. I was hoping for a C-141 Starlifter jet cargo plane. There were 10 on the list and I got the last one. This set me up for a 40-year career in aviation.

Ken Alm

April 10, 1970 we marched on the Laredo AFB parade ground and were given our Air Force Wings, the wings that had hung on the board in our training room for the past year. Then I drove to McGuire AFB, New Jersey.

McGuire Air Force Base

I arrived at McGuire AFB in April 1970 ready to learn about the C-141 and my first real assignment in a squadron. I began to feel like an Air Force Officer. I moved into the Bachelor Officers Quarters and reported to the 30th Military Airlift Squadron. I was told that my first assignment was to go to survival training at Fairchild AFB near Spokane, Washington. Survival was putting it mildly.

Survival Training: I thought pilot training was grueling, but in many respects it was pleasant compared to survival training. I had just received my pilot's wings, but was told on arrival at survival training that if I didn't pass this course then I would lose them.

It started out pleasant enough. We had academic courses to teach us what our parents told us never to do. The training was focused on what we would need to know if we were shot down or in some other way captured by the enemy. In these circumstances, you were supposed to lie, cheat, and steal to survive.

After the academics, we were handed a stick at about 9:00 one night and told to cross a field longer than a football field in the dark without being captured or killed. We wouldn't actually be killed, but there were trip wires throughout the field and if you tripped one a blast would occur on a pole above your head and an instructor would come and declare you dead. That was why you had a stick. You were supposed to wave the stick in front of you while you crawled through the field letting the stick find the trip wires so you could avoid them.

In the end, you were captured whether you made it safely to the end or not, and thrown into a Vietnam type prisoner retention and interrogation center. The interrogations were not fun, but they were instructive because you learned about how you naturally react to such circumstances and developed personal strategies that you could use if ever in that position. After a day or two (who knew what day or time it was), we were released into a WWII type POW camp where we were told that we should try to escape. All of these concepts had been taught to us in academics prior to the field exercises.

After the enemy-capture training, we had some time to recover during another round of training which taught us how to survive in the forest. This made the training we received at ROTC Summer Camp at Dover, AFB look like a picnic. No beating chickens on the ground here.

We created our backpacks and made a tent and other items out of parachute material, then set out into the virgin forest near Spokane. The objective was to follow our compass to a prearranged location about three days away. We travelled in small groups of about 8 but linked up with the larger group at night. My pack weighed 40 pounds and I weighed 125 pounds so it was quite a load for me. As we went through the woods we would come upon trees that were lying across our path. Some trees were 36 inched in diameter and 200 feet long. The trunk was often not resting on the ground so I would have to climb up 4-5 feet to get over the tree. This was difficult for me and it resulted in slowing our group down. Then, one of the resourceful members of our party had an idea. I would approach the tree backwards and two of the guys would throw my pack over the tree with me attached. This resulted in my falling to the ground on the other side on top of the pack. The pack broke my fall and gave me a reasonably soft landing. This way we could keep moving and make our night camp at a reasonable time.

Food was another issue. We were issued two pemmican bars, a potato, and an apple to eat for the three days. That and of course whatever else we could trap or find along the way.

With all the exercise we were getting most of the group was feeling starved by the third day. The last night in camp I was in a parachute tent with a navigator from Maine. My size and weight was an advantage when it came to eating. My tent-mate wasn't so lucky. He was larger and heavier so he felt the hunger more than I did. As we were lying on our backs side by side in the tent he began to moan. I knew that this was the time I had been waiting for.

Before going to survival training I had a few days at home to prepare. They had given us a uniform to wear during the training and a list of things we should bring with us. It was also clear that we would be captured and have forest survival training to contend with. I thought that it would be prudent to hide some food in my cloths to help me face the hunger and persevere. My mother sewed a candy bar into my shirttail where it would be unlikely to be discovered. As I lay beside my tent-mate I quietly whispered into his ear...."I have a Hershey bar".

He couldn't believe it. I ripped the lining out of my shirttail and there it was. Flattened from my trips over the trees on the trail, and melted from the exertion we had had, but still in the wrapper. We were like a couple of miner's looking at a hunk of gold. We both took a sniff. Yes, chocolate. Our next challenge was to open the wrapper without attracting the attention of the fellows in the other tents. Carefully, very carefully we removed the paper and opened the foil. This little bit of blissful nourishment meant the world to us and gave us the strength to finish the course. It is interesting how a little thing can change a person's mindset and give them strength.

About three weeks after we had finished the training and had returned to our home bases I received a notice that there was a package at the base post office. I went to see what it was and discovered that my friend from Maine had sent me a shore dinner with lobsters, clams, corn, etc. and a note thanking me for not just going off into the woods to eat my candy bar alone. He told me how meaningful it was for him to share my food, and friendship. It was more joyous for the sharing.

C-141 Training: I returned to McGuire AFB only to be sent to Altus AFB Oklahoma for C-141 school. Altus at that time was a cow town with a stockyard, the Horseshoe Bar, and Altus AFB. The base Officer's Club was the center of social life and all the students would go there for dinner every night. I'll never forget the sign that someone put over the entrance to the Club, "The food must me good here. A million flies cannot be wrong".

The training consisted of academics, procedures training, simulator and flight training. We would go through this training with a buddy. My buddy was Randy Rohman who I had gone through Pilot training with at Laredo AFB. Randy and I were like Mutt and Jeff. He was over 6 foot tall and I wasn't.

It was a thrill to see the 141 up close knowing that I was going to be flying the plane. It was a big four-engine jet with plenty of power. The crew consisted of and aircraft commander (AC) who sat in the left pilots seat, a copilot who sat in the right seat, a navigator, who was also an officer, sat sideways behind the AC and two flight engineers who were senior master sergeants. One flight engineer at a time sat at his instrument panel sideways behind the copilot with his back to the navigator. Down a ladder in the cargo bay were two airmen loadmasters who were usually fresh out of high school. All in all, the 141 had a diverse crew under the command of the AC.

Simulator training was the first time I had a chance to see what the cockpit was really like and get a chance to get the feel of the aircraft. The simulator had a six-axis motion system and visual system that was a nighttime digital scene with dots of lights resembling the runways, taxiways, buildings and cities.

After learning standard procedures it was time for emergency procedures.

Me on the steps of the C-141

Everything that had or could ever go wrong with the airplane was covered in this course of training. One of the parts of the training was a double engine failure on the same side of the aircraft at the worst time this could happen, just after lift-off on takeoff. At this stage of flight the plane would be it's heaviest and because you are close to the ground there was little time for corrective action. As the instructor failed the engines, the plane would yaw toward the failed engines requiring the pilot to apply full rudder and lower the nose of the aircraft to keep from stalling. As the plane gains altitude, you could retract the gear and climb to an altitude where you could refer to the checklist, deal with the emergency, and circle back to land. All this time the pilot is holding full rudder. That caused me a bit of a problem. The rudder pressure required was substantial which was no problem for a while, but after some time my rudder leg started to shake.

During training we were told that while acting as the AC we should take advantage of all the resources available to us. Then it struck me. I could direct my copilot to hold the rudder while I flew the plane and dealt with the emergency causing the engines to quit. So, as my leg started to shake I looked over at Randy and said, "Right Rudder Igor" and Randy saved the day.

Bank Robbery: During our time at Altus we had one long weekend when we were free. There were 141s going back and forth from Altus to McGuire where I was based so I invited Randy to hop a ride and come to McGuire with me for some fun. Another pilot training friend, Bob Szul, had a sister, Eileen, who lived with her folks in Trenton, NJ near McGuire. I called her to see if she would like to go out with Randy and find me a date as well. She agreed and we were all set to go out Saturday night. We were to pick up the girls at 5:30 Saturday night. I had borrowed a car from another pilot training friend who was based at McGuire. Randy and I set off from my apartment for our rendezvous in Trenton.

As we were driving up route 130 I saw a police car a good ways behind me with its lights flashing. I glanced at the speedometer and amazingly I was going under the speed limit. So I thought that they were going to pass me, but they didn't. Once I realized that they were stopping me, I pulled over, got out of the car and faced the police car. What I saw took me immediately back to my survival-training course. The two policemen barreled out of their car, one with a sawed off shotgun and the other with an M-16 riffle. One of the policemen shouted, "hands up and up against the car". Of course I complied. As the guy with the shotgun came up behind me I could see how nervous he was. He kept raising the gun up and down. I was stunned and finally said, "Was I speeding officer?" With this he ordered Randy out of the car and told him to put his hands on the hood as well. As we stood there, the other officer shouted from the police car, "It's not them Harry". With that the guy with the shotgun turned and started back to the police car. I turned and said, " Wait a minute. What is this all about?" He turned back and said that there had been a bank robbery and the robber's getaway car matched our description. "But you aren't them." We arrived at the girl's house about a half hour late. We explained that it wasn't our fault because we were stopped for bank robbery and hopped that they would forgive us. They said that they had never heard a line like THAT before. That certainly got the evening off to a great start.

I passed 141 training and returned to McGuire to begin my job as a copilot.

Flying the C-141 on Active Duty: What a joy to fly the C-141. It had a large cockpit with bunks at the rear and a cargo bay that held pallets on metal bases that could slide out for airdrops or be loaded onto K-loaders at the aerial-ports. It could also be configured with passenger seats and with lines of stretchers for medical evacuation (medevac) missions.

My first flight as a copilot was actually on a Presidential mission. It was called my dollar ride, because the tradition is that at the end of a copilot's first mission he is to give the AC a dollar. This mission was to take President Nixon's car and support equipment to Shannon Ireland. This was not only my first flight as a copilot, but my first trip to Europe as well. It was fabulous. And, I got to make the landing at Shannon airport. Dirty Nellie's pub near the airport was a real treat. I got to mingle with the locals in the bar. One of whom told me that the cost of living went up 5% because that is how much the price of beer had risen.

McGuire had several standard missions that were flown each month. There was the run to the east. This typically included flying from McGuire to Frankfort Germany, to Turkey, to Tehran, to Addis Ababa Ethiopia and back through either

Athens, Greece or Madrid, Spain. Occasionally we would go to Greenland, Iceland or England. The eastbound trips would generally take about 10 days. We would fly to the first destination and go into 16 hours of crew rest while another crew took our plane on to its next destination. This is called staging because the planes never stopped for long while the crews were staged across the system.

When we returned to McGuire we would have a couple of days off, then we would be sent west. This was at the height of the Viet Nam war, so that is where we were headed. The typical flight for us would be from McGuire to Anchorage, Alaska, to Yokota Japan, to one of the bases in Viet Nam and back to Kadena AFB on Okinawa. From there we would shuttle back and forth into the war zone, finally returning to McGuire through Alaska again. Most of the time we would only get 16 hours on the ground between flights, giving us enough time to have a meal and explore the vicinity near the base. Occasionally, the plane behind us would not be coming for another day so we would get 24 or more hours off to explore the surroundings. What an incredible experience for a 25 year old to explore Europe and Asia.

The C-141 had one of the most amazing views in aviation. As I sat in the pilot's seat I had a 180-degree view out the front of the aircraft. Huge picture windows all around showed me unbelievable sites. We would glide over European cities at night seeing the white lights of the buildings and the orange lights of the super highways. We would glide over the tops of the mountains in Alaska as we descended into Anchorage. Mt. Fuji is an incredible site from the air. One night I was flying out from Goose Bay Labrador over the ocean heading to Lands End in England when we saw the northern lights below us to the north. These are sights that I shall never forget.

Another incredible thing about flying the C-141 was the shopping. Imagine flying a cargo aircraft all around the world. You could bring anything back as long as it wasn't hazardous, adversely affected the mission, or would be prohibited by customs. It was a hard decision whether to buy my stereo in Germany or Japan. At this time the dollar was doing better than other currencies so everything seemed inexpensive compared to the U.S. I brought back a papasan chair and hibachi pot from Japan, Hummels and crystal glasses from Germany, Persian rugs from Iran, jewelry from Thailand, and Roman oil lamps and copper pots from Turkey. Everyone used to joke that my apartment was decorated in early MAC (Military Airlift Command). The hardest parts of leaving the C-141 were the flying, my friends in the unit, and the shopping.

After a year of flying as a copilot I upgraded to Aircraft Commander (AC). It was a blessing for me to be trained by ACs that had flown during the Korean War and had thousands of hours of flight experience. By the following year I was an instructor and flight examiner. Then I was teaching a group of pilots who were only about a year or two younger than me so part of my challenge was to pass on what I had been taught. This became critical on a flight into Addis Ababa, Ethiopia.

Addis Ababa, Ethiopia: I was awakened at the International Hotel in Tehran, Iran by the Airlift Operations Center (Ops). They told me that the bus would come to pick up my crew in about an hour for our flight to Addis Ababa, Ethiopia. The U.S. was friendly with Iran at the time because the Shaw was still in power. I went down to the restaurant, had breakfast, and we went to Base Ops to file our flight plan and check the cargo for our trip to Addis. All went well and we departed on our flight. We had two copilots on board that made us an augmented crew so that we could fly longer than normal.

As we reached altitude, I started to feel ill. It was the orange juice. Don't eat fresh fruit or drink fresh orange juice in Iran. Fortunately the C-141 has a toilet, so I headed there thinking that would be the end of my suffering, but it wasn't. I headed to the bunk while the two copilots took the helm. I told them to get me up an hour prior to our descent so that we could discuss the landing and hopefully by then I would feel better. I didn't feel better, but I felt that I needed to make the approach and landing because of that particular airport.

Addis Ababa airport is 7,631 feet high in the mountains. At that altitude the aircraft does not respond as quickly and needs more power during the approach because the air is less dense. The runway starts at the end of a shear cliff. I knew from previous flights that the cliff was littered with aircraft wreckage from planes that had hit the cliff below the runway and crashed down the hillside. I didn't want that to be us. So I got into the pilot's seat and began the descent. I quickly realized that I did not have the strength to manipulate the controls so I asked the copilot to return to my seat. I sat on the jump seat instructing the copilots as we made the approach. During the approach to the runway we started to descend below the glide path..."More power...More power," I shouted. We landed safely and I went off to the hospital in an ambulance.

A day later, after IVs and medication, I was released to go to the hotel where my crew was staying. They were out exploring and I was told that our flight would not depart until the next day. I went up to the front desk and asked what was around that I might enjoy seeing. They told me that I was in luck; this was the day of the Mercato -- the open-air market that is held once a month in Addis Ababa. The Mercato is the largest open-air market in Africa, covering several square miles and employing an estimated 13,000 people in 7,100 business entities. I wanted to go, but how?

As I left the hotel, I was greeted by two African college students who introduced themselves to me in perfect English. They asked if I needed a tour guide. I said that I wanted to go to the Mercato, but didn't know the way. They told me how wonderful the Mercato is and that they would take me in a taxi and show me around. Being half astute, I said that I knew that their offer was not simply out of the goodness of their hearts and that I wanted to make a deal before we left, not after. They said that they would like American cloths so if I had a pair of blue jeans or a tee shirt that would be great. I told them they had a deal and we jumped into a cab.

They were right. What a sight. Colorful clothing, smells of spices and fruit, unbelievable sites. For example, there was a field that was bigger than a football field with women sitting behind peddle sewing machines, sewing. Another field with blankets covered with spices caught my eye. Together, a mass of people from different tribes were selling, bartering and buying. It turned out that my two college student guides were from different tribes. They showed me how the different pattern of scars on their faces would tell them apart. I felt somewhat secure because it became apparent that they could only talk to each other in English so I could understand their discussion.

After walking around for some time they asked me what I wanted to buy and started listing things. At one point they listed animal skins. Well, that was something I would not have thought of, and didn't really want, but I thought it might be interesting to see what was being sold. They began to lead me toward some buildings off to my left. Next thing I knew a door was opened and I was inside. That is when it hit me... I was now in a nearly dark room, in a building with people I didn't really know, and no one knew where I was.

As my eyes adapted to the light I could see that the room was two stories high covered in animal skins. The only light was coming from two small windows on the second floor. One of my guides started talking in his native tongue. The next thing I saw was a man approaching me to inquire what kind of skins I was interested in. My guide translated. I, of course, had no idea so I said how about lions, tigers, or bears? He told me that these were either not from Africa or were endangered species. I asked what he had and he began to show me antelope and other various species. It might have been my imagination, but I felt that my life could depend on my buying something. I could picture myself on the wall of the building. At that point he pulled out a round rug that was black with white tufts. I asked him what kind of fur it was. He told me monkey. This looked like the best of the lot so I went for it. I stood before him and told him that I loved it, took out my wallet, opened it and took all the money out of it and said, "is this enough to buy this?" I had about $35 and while that was probably much more than the rug should have cost, I wanted to make it clear to everyone in the room that this was all the money I had. At that point, he took the money, wrapped up the rug, and gave it to me. I thanked him and told my guides that it was time to return to the hotel. As I was leaving, the man came up to me and said he had a gift for me. It was a monkey-tail-fly-chaser. It was a white tuft of monkey tail on the end of a stick about a foot long that was wrapped with brightly colored twine. The idea is that as a fly comes near you, you can swish it away with the monkey tail.

We finally emerged into the light and found a cab to take me back to the hotel. I had to go inside to get some cash to give the taxi driver and the cloths I had agreed to give my guides. As it turned out, I had an amazing adventure and all appeared to be on the up and up. However, I decided then and there that I would not put myself into a situation like that again.

AF Reserves: After four and a half years of active duty, I transferred to an Associate Reserve Squadron, the $335^{th.}$ It was the sister squadron of the 30th active duty squadron. The idea was that the reserve squadron would merge with the active duty squadron in times of war. I became a Department of Defense (DoD) GS-13 Instructor Pilot for the 335th and was one of four pilots who were full time employees who ran the squadron day to day. They call this position an Air Reserve Technician (ART). One of the requirements was to also be a member of the squadron so you had all the same flight training and operating requirements as the pilots in the squadron, but day to day worked in the office, performed local training for the reservists, and administered check rides to evaluate their performance. In addition, the position offered the squadron some flexibility to support members who had civilian jobs. If a reservist didn't show up for a flight he was scheduled to take for some reason, then one of the four pilot ARTs was to fill in. This made life very uncertain for me. You could go to work one day with plans to go out to dinner after work and end up flying to Frankfurt on a ten day trip.

When I joined the Reserves I had the opportunity to fly with many talented people who were successful beyond their reserve flying. I was blessed by becoming good friends with a reservist navigator who was a baritone opera singer when not on active duty. His name was Paul Jan Kotula. We formed a bond and flew a lot together. He would go to the back of the aircraft and practice for his next performance. He said that the cargo bay was great acoustically. So once we were out over the ocean and he had taken his position fixes and sent the position report to air traffic control he would go to the back and sing. Talk about surreal. I would be sitting in the pilot's seat looking out over the ocean at 37,000 feet listening to an opera sung live.

One trip we were on together took us to the town of Bury St. Edmonds in England. It had a church where the Magna Carta was posted in 1214. Outside the church is a park. Paul and I went to a market shop to get a sandwich at lunchtime and sat in the park on a beautiful summer day, eating, and watching the people walk by. After we finished our lunch, Paul got up and began to sing. His voice filled the square and the people flocked to see who was singing. He finished, they clapped and we went toward the train station to go back to our base. I am very sad to say that Paul died of a brain aneurysm at age 33. If he hadn't, you would have heard of him.

Goosebay: Most of our missions were fairly routine. The old saying is, "hours and hours of shear boredom separated by moments of stark terror." I was fortunate not to experience the latter except on one trip.

About once a year or so the base would undergo an Operationally Readiness Inspection (ORI). During an ORI, inspectors from Headquarters MAC (now Air Mobility Command AMC) would descend on the base unannounced and begin observing the operation. The base and its commanders were graded on the outcome of the inspection which would last several days. The day the ORI hit McGuire I was scheduled to fly a medevac mission from McGuire to Frankfurt with a stop in Goosebay, Labrador, Canada. I arrived at the base about 6PM to begin my flight planning and was told about the ORI. I discovered that the weather was terrible all up and down the east coast of New England and eastern Canada. I decided to add some extra fuel to the mission for added safety. When I got out to the plane the fueling trucks were pulling away and I was met by a Colonel. He asked me why I wanted more fuel. I told him of the weather and he told me that our flight would be delayed if we waited to get the additional fuel. This would be a black mark for the base during the inspection. He pressured me to take the plane and if need be divert anywhere we needed in order to get more fuel as long as we took off from McGuire on time. After much discussion I finally agreed to make the on-time departure.

As I boarded the aircraft I could see lines of stretchers locked into posts from floor to ceiling in the cargo deck. The stretchers held patients, many with IVs, who were being flown back to Germany with family members and nurses. I realized how serious it was to make this flight as smooth as possible.

We took off and headed up the east coast in the darkness. I asked the navigator to monitor fuel and identify alternates where the weather was good so that we would be able to divert if fuel got low or the weather at our destination became a problem. Goosebay was calling for 2,000-foot ceilings and 2 miles visibility. That was not great, but not a problem for an instrument approach. As we proceeded north, we began to check the weather at other airports including Gander and St. Johns, both were below our minimum approach weather, but Goosebay was still fine. Finally it was decision time for diverting or pressing on. I decided to press on because the weather we were receiving from Goosebay was good and my desire to not make the trip more difficult for my passengers. That was a mistake.

Charles H. Huettner

As we started our approach to Goosebay, the weather seemed terrible at altitude. We contacted Goosebay approach control and they told us that we would receive a GCA approach. During a GCA instrument approach the radar controller talks you down from watching your aircraft on his radar. He begins by giving you a heading and watches your track on the radar. If you start to drift left of course he tells you to turn right a few degrees and watches some more. Eventually he is able to give you a heading that keeps you on track. When you get to the point where you need to descend he says, "Begin descent". The pilot then pulls back the power and lowers the nose of the aircraft about 3 degrees establishing about a 600 foot per minute descent. The controller then advises to increase or decrease the pitch to keep the aircraft on the glide slope at the appropriate speed. The pilot flies the plane and the copilot monitors the instruments and looks for the runway. The course and descent corrections continue until the aircraft gets to the decision-height, the altitude above the ground where the pilot either sees the approach lights and lands visually or initiates a go-around for another approach. This is what was happening that night with all the patients and families in the back.

Turn left, stop turn, begin descent, turn further left, stop turn, turn further left.... As we approached the decision height the copilot shouted there is the runway! I looked up and saw nothing. Then he pointed. The runway was out the right side copilot's window. I was tracking about 40 degrees from the runway heading to stay on course. I turned toward the runway with the ailerons and stepped on the opposite rudder to, as they say, "slip" the aircraft to a heading that would make it possible to land. Aircraft don't land well sideways. I did not have enough control to fight the wind and drifted left of the runway causing me to go around. To make matters worse, there was blowing snow requiring our engine and wing anti-ice protection to be on (which burns more fuel). As we went around the navigator informed me that we did not have enough fuel to divert to another airport with better weather. We had to land. I must admit that just writing this description has caused me to break out into a sweat again.

As we climbed to make another approach I asked approach control to change the runway to the other end so that the runway would be outside my window instead of the copilots. This took some time, and fuel, but it was my only chance at making the landing. Because we were flying at low altitude with all the anti-icing on we had enough fuel for about two more attempts. Turn right, begin descent, turn further right, turn further right.... we made the next approach. The crew was hushed. We all knew that our lives depended on my ability to safely land the plane. This time the copilot yelled runway in sight and pointed out the left window. I turned and slipped the plane again. It took all the rudder I had and the yoke was almost to the stops. The cross controls and the slippery runway did the trick. This time I was able to land and continue to fly the plane on the ice until we were able to slow down enough to taxi off the runway.

As I emerged from the cockpit I saw all the families and medical workers exiting to get some dinner in the terminal. I began to shake. The passengers had no idea of what had just transpired. I was angry. I went directly to Goosebay tower to speak to the controllers. "Why did you send out false weather reports and risk all our lives? How could you do such a thing??" Their response was that we were carrying their mail and they hadn't received mail for over a week due to poor weather. They knew that we would not land there if we knew the real weather report. I reported this to the unit commander with my recommendation that someone get court-martialed. I also learned an important lesson about being bullied into taking a flight or doing something when I know it to be wrong. I learned that when that kind of pressure is on me to just say no.

Mugged: Many of our missions departed McGuire late at night. This required me to be tired during the day so I could sleep prior to my reporting for duty at midnight. One day, I set the alarm to get up early and decided to take my bike to a bike path along the Schuylkill River in Philadelphia. I was living in Burlington, N.J. at the time and liked going to Philadelphia, it was not too far away. I had an old Chevy van that I used to transport my bike. I threw the bike into the van and set off for the park hoping that a good brisk ride would tire me out so I could sleep prior to my flight.

   I parked my van a ways down the bike path and started to ride toward the city. The river was on my right and a hillside that goes up to the Museum of Art was on my left. A beautiful ride and no one around or so I thought. As I came close to the boathouses there was a huge bolder that went across the road to the water. The bolder has a hole in it for the road and cars to travel through. The bike path is built out from the rock and goes around it on the riverside. I started to go around the rock when I saw a large black guy standing in the middle of the path. I came to a stop to avoid hitting him when he grabbed me by the shirt and said, "Give me your money and your watch". I couldn't believe that this was happening to me. I was really stuck. The bike was between my legs and he was pushing me against the wall that dropped to the river. I tried to delay by fussing with my wallet and he shouted to his accomplice who was standing on top of the bolder looking both ways to ensure that no one was coming. No one was. He then grabbed my watch by its metal band and started to pull it off my wrist. Now his left hand had me by the shirt and his right had was on the watch. We tugged at each other for a moment or two and I said, "Look, I know you need money. I'll trade you my wallet for my watch." To my surprise he agreed and let go of my watch. As I continued to delay getting my wallet out my back pocket he reared back to hit me. I then immediately presented my wallet. He grabbed it and climbed up the rock to escape. When he reached the top of the rock I called out to him. I said, "No hard feelings. Please take the money and throw my wallet back so I can have my driver's license. " He did.

I struggled to turn my bike around and race back to my van. This would normally be the end of the story, but it was just the beginning. As I was peddling back, a police car came up the parkway with two police officers. I flagged them down. "I've been mugged!" I shouted. I told the officers what happened and one of them asked me if I would help him find my mugger. I agreed, so he put my bike in the trunk of the police car and put me in the back seat. We circled around up the hill where my assailant had run. This began my two-hour police ordeal.

We began by going up to a city swimming pool on top of the hill. The officers asked me to walk into the pool area and if I spotted the mugger to simply point at him. I told them that I didn't think this was a good idea, but they insisted. I was the only white person fully dressed walking into a swimming pool area where everyone was black and in bathing suits. To make matters worse there were two white police officers following me. I took a quick look around and headed for the door. They stopped me and insisted that I look in the locker room. I told them that I appreciated that they were trying to help me, but I was ready to go back to my van.

We pressed on driving through the park near the pool. At one point we emerged from the woods at a softball field to see a group of black guys playing softball. A police car driving through the woods certainly caught their attention. The game stopped and the senior player who was about 18 years old or so came up to the car. He looked in and saw me in the back seat. He obviously thought that they had caught me. He and his group started to rock the car and shout, "Let the white kid go, let the white kid go!" With that the officers threw open the doors and confronted the kids. The senior player continued his refrain. With that the officer grabbed the kid and shoved his head into the open door of the car and said to me, " Is this the guy? Is this the guy?" I said no. He asked again. I said no again. He then said, "In a minute this is going to be the guy." I told the officer, "over my dead body" and the officer let the kid go. After this we drove the streets and at one point drove over a railroad bridge. Finally they took me to the police station to file a report. As I was doing so, I asked the sergeant in the station why they went to so much trouble for my $30 robbery? He told me that there had been a murder on top of the hill the previous night and they thought this might be connected. I am sure that it wasn't.

They finally told me I was free to go, but I didn't even know where I was at that point. Eventually they drove me back to my van with my bike and I started back to my apartment. This sort of adventure was certainly not conducive to my resting before my flight, but I was happy to still have my watch and wallet and be free of the long arm of the law.

To get to my apartment I had to cross the Burlington-Bristol Bridge. As I approached the bridge, I remembered that I didn't have any money. The bridge toll was 5 cents. I approached the tollbooth and told the toll collector my story. He frowned and demanded the money. I opened the ashtray in the van and found five pennies that had been spray painted in the bottom. I pried them out and handed them to the toll-master. I was on my way home to rest.

Exciting Missions: One of my most exciting missions was during the 1973 Arab-Israeli War. America supported Israel from Arab invaders when no one else would. This involved continuous supply flights between America and Tel Aviv airport. The US Air Force set up a stage at Lajas AFB in the Azores and all MAC crews were pressed into service. An augmented crew would take off from Lajas and fly down the middle of the Mediterranean Sea along the airspace boundary between Europe and Africa. As we came close to the coast of Africa approaching the Middle East, Israeli F-4 fighter jets would fly formation with us to escort us to the airport. It was an amazing site to look out the side window and see a fighter with a blue Star of David on the nose off our wing. We would wave to their pilots and they would salute back.

When we landed in Tel Aviv our engineers would refuel the plane, the loadmasters would unload the cargo, and the pilots and navigators would go into the terminal. After filing our flight plan for the return trip we were ushered into a room and served dinner by the El Al flight attendants. While we ate we were given letters from a large mail sack to read. They were from Israeli school children that had written to thank the American pilots for saving their lives. This was so emotional that it was hard to eat. When the plane was offloaded and refueled it was time to go. The objective was to keep the plane on the ground as little time as possible so that the next could arrive and our plane could be recycled as quickly as possible. It is an experience I will never forget.

Another highlight of my military flying career was transporting cargo to Antarctica. This was called a Deep Freeze mission. MAC bases and crews lobbied hard to be able to take one of these missions. We took off from McGuire with two augmented crews. An augmented crew contained three pilots so that one could always be resting. We flew from McGuire to Hawaii then on to Christ Church, New Zealand. It was Christmas time when spring was turning to summer below the equator. The mission was to supply the scientists at the US station at McMurdo Sound. There is a brief period of time when the ice is beginning to melt. During this time the C-130s are too small to bring in enough supplies yet the ice is not thin enough for the icebreaker ships to get to the station. We set up our own stage out of Christ Church. One augmented crew would fly down and back one day and the other would do the same the next. We did this for about a week. This gave each crew a day every other day to enjoy Christ Church and get two trips to the ice.

The mission was a real experience. It began with a flight plan that contained a "point of no return". This was the point in the flight when you were committed to land on the ice because there would not be enough fuel to fly to an alternate airport. The weather in Antarctica is unpredictable. Storms crop up quickly and blow snow to the point where there can be zero visibility. The runway was a plowed section of ice that ran for miles with makeshift lights on the edge. Because the runway was ice, it was very difficult to see in blowing snow. If the forecast turned grim prior to the point of no return we could turn around and return to Christ Church. After that point, we had to land on the ice.

To make maters worse, we had to fly in compass grid. When you are close to the poles, the magnetic compasses are inaccurate so the navigator had to rely on star shots and a computer that was not getting input from the magnetic compass. If you can believe this, in the days before GPS, the navigator actually had a periscope type device that would stick out of the top of the aircraft and provide him with a way to see the stars, identify our location, and determine our track across the ground / water. As we approached McMurdo we would contact approach control and they would vector us for a GCA approach as I described previously. If a whiteout occurred we were to set up a 600 foot per minute descent and wait to touchdown. Hopefully the runway would be long and wide enough to allow a safe landing. Fortunately, I never experienced a white out.

As we got off the aircraft at McMurdo station we saw a series of buildings, a few emperor penguins, and personnel dressed in orange parkas. America has been conducting research in Antarctica for many years. As a result, the buildings were almost below ground / snow level. As time went buy, more snow fell on top, and the heat of the buildings caused them to sink into the ice below. To get into the door of the building you would descend a set of snow steps to a carved out landing. This is where we went to get to the café and to file our flight plan for the return flight at base operations. After offloading our cargo and refueling, we took off for our trip back to Christ Church. As we departed we flew around the inactive volcano near the station. What a view!

Back in Christ Church we had a great time. We met some locals about our age who were interested in what we were doing and happy for us to join in on their holiday parties. The women were beautiful and the guys were good blokes who impressed us by opening beer bottles with their teeth.

On Christmas day our entire crew went to a fancy restaurant near our hotel. They had a fixed price dinner that was unbelievable. They gave us the regular menu and told us that we could order anything we wanted and as much as we wanted. We started with an order of all the appetizers and went from there. It was certainly a meal to remember. Finally, it was New Years Eve and I had managed to get a date with one of the local girls. My excitement turned grim when I got the word that we were alerted to return to the States. How could they do this to us? I called back to ensure that this wasn't a joke, but the orders were real. I had to break the news to my crew who also had plans that needed to be broken.

So there we were a few hours before midnight heading back to Hickam AFB in Hawaii. As we progressed on our flight a thought occurred to us. We were going to cross the international dateline so we would have one more chance at New Years Eve. Not the party we planned, but an opportunity for a party none-the-less. The end of the story was not a happy one. We were alerted again for a 10:00 PM flight from Hickam to return to McGuire. We had the potential of two New Year's Eves and lost them both.

Commanders Call: As my time as an Air Reserve Technician came toward a close we had a real problem to face. The Air Force was retrofitting the C-141 with inertial navigation systems and better computers that could calculate and program our flight path. This was very unsettling for the navigators because this is what they were trained to do. They could see the writing on the wall that they were being replaced by technology. As the tensions rose in the unit, we arranged for a management meeting with our reserve Squadron Commander prior to the squadron's monthly Commander's Call meeting. We told the Commander that we needed him to calm the fears of the navigators at the Commander's Call. He told us that he would take care of it and went out to speak to the squadron. After discussing the other issues of the day, he cleared his throat and addressed the navigators. This is what he said. "Now I know that you navigators are upset and concerned that the new equipment will jeopardize your jobs. You shouldn't be concerned. What if we need to fly somewhere where there aren't any coordinates?" This did not calm the navigators.

Pentagon

In 1975, I left my ART position and began my career with the FAA. In 1979, I transitioned from the Air Force Reserve Unit I just described to a position called an "Individual Mobilization Augmentee" (IMA). IMA's are Air Force Reservists who are assigned to augment an active duty organization rather than serving in a Reserve Unit. I, therefore, continued to be in the AF Reserves while working at the FAA. I was assigned to an active duty organization in the Pentagon, office symbol XOOTD, that was responsible for Air Force flight training and simulation policy. This was a great assignment for me because I was working on flight simulator regulations for the FAA at the same time. I could share insights between the military and civil aviation authorities.

Once a year the AF Reserves would hold a session for the reservist IMA's who worked in the operations part of the Pentagon. We would receive briefings that would give us a bigger picture view of what was happening outside of our particular office. These annual sessions began with everyone introducing him or herself and each participant describing what civilian jobs we had.

One year during the introductions a new Captain introduced himself as Ross Perot Junior with a job in real estate. It was great to get to know Ross. He told us stories of his around the world helicopter trip and how Oliver North, who was a staffer in the White House at the time, helped him get the country clearances he needed to make the trip. During one of these sessions, Ross and I went to lunch together. I asked him if he wanted to go to the Base Exchange before lunch. He said that he didn't need anything. That struck me as obviously true. We shared a pizza together and when the bill came we decided to split the cost. It was an odd number of dollars and I offered to pay the extra dollar. Ever since, I have been able to jokingly say that the Ross Perot owes me money.

I spent a total of 19 years at the Pentagon ending up in the office of the Air Force Chief of Safety (SE). I was fortunate that General Jack Cole was the Chief. His position had recently been moved from Kirtland AFB in Albuquerque, NM to the Pentagon and he was looking for an IMA. By that time, I was the Deputy Associate Administrator for Safety at the FAA so I was a perfect match. We worked extremely well together and became great friends after he left the service. I owe it to him for helping me become a Colonel and for making connections between the USAF and FAA that helped improve safety of both civil and military fleets.

After several years working in the safety office the Chief of Safety was elevated to a two star and moved back to Kirtland. That left the office in the Pentagon with an active duty Colonel in command. It's a long story, but through a pilot friend of mine, Jim Coziahr, I was introduced to the Air Force Chief of Staff at the time, General Ron Fogleman. General Fogleman is one of the most straight forward, honest, talented, and patriotic people that I have ever known. I had the opportunity to discuss with him the idea that he could create an IMA one-star position in the AF safety office that would report to the two-star at Kirtland. This way the AF would have an AF Reserve general officer stationed in DC who could effectively also connect with the FAA. He liked the idea and began the personnel process to establish the one-star position. I was in perfectly qualified to successfully compete for the position as FAA's Acting Associate Administrator for Aviation Safety. Then it happened.

Here is what happened next as told by Dr. Richard H. Kohn[i].

On Monday, 28 July 1997, Gen Ronald R. Fogleman asked Secretary of the Air Force Sheila Widnall to be relieved of his duties as chief of staff of the Air Force and retired as soon as possible, a year before the end of his four-year term. At the time, the press and electronic media overwhelmingly interpreted General Fogleman's act as a resignation in protest over the secretary of defense's intention to block the promotion of Brig Gen Terryl "Terry" Schwalier to Major General. Schwalier had commanded the 4404th Composite Wing in Saudi Arabia the previous year when a terrorist bomb had destroyed the Air Force housing complex known as Khobar Towers outside Dhahran Air Base, killing 19 airmen and wounding a total of some three hundred Americans. After one Department of Defense (DOD) and two Air Force investigations, Fogleman had concluded that Schwalier had done everything that could be expected of a commander and had no culpability in the tragedy; punishing him would have a chilling effect on commanders around the world that might then infer that protecting their forces outweighed accomplishing their missions.

General Fogleman was gone and so was my promotion.

Chapter 4: Home

Met Kathie: While I was on active duty my parents wanted to stay in touch, so they asked me to call them on Wednesdays and Sundays. We would talk about what was going on with them and I would tell them about my Air Force adventures. It was a really good way to stay close. As I described earlier, I was flying around the world and my folks got wanderlust. My great grandfather had come to America from Germany at age 14 in 1868 and no member of the family had ever been back. My father said, "If you can go to Europe, then so should we". I offered to plan a trip for us, but they opted for an American Express Alpine bus tour.

We flew from JFK Airport to Frankfurt where they loaded us on a bus and took us to the castle in Heidelberg, Germany. The day ended in the wine cellar where we met the others on the tour. That is where I met Kathie and Linda. Kathie and I hit it off almost immediately. Linda was a vivacious honey blond who was traveling with Kathie and who was out to meet European men. This resulted in Kathie and I sitting on the bus behind my folks and Linda sitting with others on the tour. I believe my folks were a bit disappointed in my change of focus from them to Kathie, but the result was that our first date lasted two weeks as we toured the Alps.

As we reached the hotel our first night an incredible thing happened. As we stood in the lobby to register, several of the men on the hotel staff approached Linda and asked her out. She declined being exhausted from the flight and tour, but it was obvious to me that she would have no problem meeting dates for the evening. Being the entrepreneur that I am and having a credential as an international traveler, I spoke to Linda the next morning to warn her of the potential problems of her going off on her own at night in a foreign country with men that she did not know. I offered her a way to achieve her goal by including Kathie and me. I suggested to her that each time we arrived at the hotel for the night, she could pick out someone she would like to go out with and see if he wanted to go. I said that she should ensure that he had a car so that she could go out on the town. I also suggested that once the date was confirmed, she should say that she needed to have Kathie and me along. In this way she had support if things got out of hand for her. This resulted in an incredible tour almost every evening provided by a local guy with a car. Imagine zooming through the streets of Vienna in a Morris Mini from disco to disco. I ensured that we all got back to the hotel before the bus left in the morning. The result was that we slept on the bus through some of the cathedral tours, but the nighttime experience was unmatched.

Kathie and Me

One particularly memorable evening was the evening we stayed in Lucerne, Switzerland. The hotel had a water taxi that went to a Northern French Riviera gambling casino. We had to go.

As we departed the boat we were ushered into a small room inside the front door of a casino that looked like it was right out of a James Bond movie. A man sat behind a desk and asked us to sit down and show him our passports. He then asked us how much credit we wanted. I replied that we would not be using credit and he opened the door for us to go into the casino. It was magical: crystal chandeliers, men in tuxedos, lines of roulette tables and a raised section of the room for baccarat. There were no slot machines, poker tables, or blackjack tables.

Susie, Joanne, Linda, Me, Kathie, Brent

After walking around the room, Linda and I picked out a roulette table. Kathie told us that she didn't want to gamble and went to watch others play. Linda took a seat near the croupier and I went to the other end of the table. We played for about a half an hour when Linda came around the table to talk to me. She said that the croupier was showing her what to bet on and at other times just scraped chips to her. I was dumbfounded and told her that it must be her imagination. She said no, telling me that the croupier would pause over a number while scraping up the chips after a round and look at her while doing this. The next round would find the ball landing on that number. It was hard to believe, but I began watching and subtly playing a column or color to align with the number he was showing Linda. The table was obviously rigged, but how?? All I can say is that he was calling the next winning number. As his time at the table ended, he went around behind Linda and quietly said to her, "I'll see you later." At that, she came running back to me. About this time it dawned on me that no one knew where we were and that we were not even in the same country as the tour. We found Kathie and made a hasty retreat to the boat.

Fast-forward about twelve years and I was sitting at a roulette table in a hotel in Addas Ababa, Ethiopia. There were two Japanese businessmen playing with piles of chips. I figured if roulette could be rigged in France imagine what could be done in Ethiopia. So, I made modest bets between the bets of the businessmen and did quite well tipping the croupier every so often. My take away lesson from these experiences is to find a roulette table where there is a lot of money on the table and bet between the heavy betters. I don't know how, but it works.

Moosonee Canada: After the two-week trip where we met, Kathie and I found that getting additional time together was difficult. Kathie was a registered nurse in the pediatric unit of a hospital on Long Island and I was on active duty at McGuire AFB in New Jersey. I was living near the base and would be away for weeks at a time. She worked the four to midnight shift with one day off a week and every other weekend. Finding the time for me to come to Long Island when she was off work was a problem.

One part of the solution was that I had a great aunt Sarah still living in Hicksville so I would arrange to stay with her and drive the 20 miles to Stony Brook where Kathie lived with her folks. The result was many months between visits. After doing this for about two years, we decided that we should take a trip together. We decided on a driving trip to Canada.

Our trip took us to Montreal, Ottawa, and Toronto in October. While in Toronto we toured the Molson Brewery. At the end of the tour our group was led into a large hall filled with round tables so we could sample the beer. We saw a single man sitting at one of the tables and decided to sit with him. He turned out to be a freelance nature writer. He asked us about our trip and we listened to some of his writing adventures. During our discussion Kathie asked him if he would recommend a route where we could see some of the Canadian countryside because we had spent our trip thus far in cities. He said that we should go to Moosonee, north of Toronto above the Arctic Circle. He told us that we needed to call the Moosonee Lodge to get a reservation because it was the only place to stay, then get train tickets up that evening and back the following day. We did as he suggested.

That evening about 9:00PM we parked our car under the railroad bridge and boarded the sleeper train heading due north. As we boarded the train, we meet a nice fellow with two young children. I had a Polaroid camera and they had never seen one. I took a picture of the kids and that began the friendship. He worked for the Canadian Bureau of Indian Affairs and was returning to Cochrane, Canada from his visit in Toronto. Our trip was to go from Toronto to Cochrane overnight then change to a narrow gage train to Moosonee. As we got on the train, our new friend suggested that we meet for a drink once we all got settled. We agreed and looked for our accommodations. It turned out that we had a top bunk in a car of two person bunk beds with curtains for privacy. Our roommate in the bunk below was a lumberjack who had cut his leg off and was now proudly sporting a new prosthesis. When he learned that Kathie was a nurse, he was anxious to show her what a good job the doctors had done on his leg. Our adventure had begun.

We finally got away from the lumberjack and looked for our Canadian friends in the bar car. As we went from car to car, we finally spotted the man and his kids sitting on one of the benches in a passenger car. We approached and asked him where we should go for our drink. He said, "Right here". With that he pulled out a half gallon of Four Roses liquor and two wax paper cups handing one to each of us. We didn't know what to say as he filled each cup to the brim. No ice, no mix, just rotgut whiskey and no place to discretely get rid of it. As I looked into the glass, I could see the wax melting off the sides and floating to the top. He began to tell us how many of the Indians were alcoholics causing him problems. I somehow didn't think it was only the Indians that had such a problem. Kathie and I did our best to choke down the fiery liquid. I finished mine with one last big gulp then crushed the glass to ensure that he wouldn't try to give me a refill. I was amazed with the kid's reaction. The young boy looked up at his father and said, " He crushed the cup Dad, now we can't use it again". So how many times had they used the cups? Well, I am sure that any germs that resided in the cup were long dead, but that was enough for us to bid our good night and return to our bunk. They would be spending the night on the bench.

We woke up in the morning to see a world of trees and snow. The train came into the station at Cochrane in the morning giving us time to explore town. Cochrane at the time was like I pictured the Wild West. There were stores and businesses on both sides of a short main street with covered wooden boardwalks as sidewalks. After checking out the few stores and Laundromat we entered a saloon with pool tables. Kathie was good at pool from her nursing training days at the VA hospital, and I had some experience from my fraternity days, so we stepped up to one of the tables and began to play. The men at the bar were not amused. I can't be sure, but we got the feeling that Kathie was the first woman who had ever set foot in the joint who didn't work there, and they didn't like me either. We finished the game and left much to the relief of all in attendance.

Soon we were aboard the train for our final leg to Moosonee. It was even more wonderful a site than our travel writer described. We looked out over wilderness populated only with animals and trappers. Along the route we saw small sheds filled with wood. As a trappers emerged from the woods they would use the wood to light a fire. When the engineer on the train saw a fire, he would stop the train and the trappers would board with their pile of pelts. Around 3:30 in the afternoon we arrived in Moosonee. Being above the Arctic Circle the light appeared to be dusk and the ground was frozen and covered with snow. We made our way to the Moosonee Lodge and checked into what appeared to be a two story 1950 frame motel with about 20 sparsely decorated rooms and a café. I could see how important it was to have a reservation in advance. We went out to explore the town. During the summer, fishermen and tourists would come to journey across a short inlet to an island where they would camp, but at that time of the year all was frozen and landlocked. Our tour of the town included the Indian school, huge liquor store, and the Hudson's Bay store. Other than the train station, a few homes and sheds, that was it. By 4:30 we had done the town and returned to the lodge. We thought we might find a place by the fire and have a drink in the bar, but there was no bar or fire (or TV or radio for that matter). Moosonee was a dry town so no selling drinks by the glass (only bottles from the liquor store that was now closed). We ended up having dinner about 5:30 and settled into our room for the night.

Charles H. Huettner

The next morning we were up early so we would not miss the train going back to Toronto. As we sat on a bench in the railroad station a trapper with an Indian squaw came and sat opposite us on a facing bench. He had a pile of pelts to his right and his Indian companion to his left. He was dressed like you would picture Davy Crockett in buckskin with fringe. She was in Indian dress and was drunk. She sat head down mumbling to herself... humm... whoooo... hummm... heee. Suddenly she jumped up, ran in front of him grabbing his rifle swinging it around the room yelling, "I'm going to kill you". Everyone in the station hit the dirt except Kathie and me. We were stunned and had the deer-in-the-headlight looks on our faces. He grabbed the rifle from her and hit her with the butt of the gun. She rolled onto the floor then returned to her seat. As people scrambled back to their feet the train arrived. Kathie and I got up and moved towards the door just as the train began to load. As we moved to the door, the Indian woman came up beside us and reached into her pocket. She pulled out what appeared to be a 4-foot long snake and shoved it in Kathie's face. Kathie shrieked and the woman laughed. It turned out to be a rubber snake, but it was totally believable that it was real. During the ride back to Toronto we calmed ourselves looking at the trees and snow. That evening we pulled into the train station in Toronto having had an adventure of a lifetime and with the sure knowledge that we could make it as a couple in spite of anything.

Haddonfield: Kathie and I were married in 1974 while I was an Air Force, Air Reserve Technician for the 335 Military Airlift Squadron. I was working at McGuire AFB as described earlier, but we wanted to live off-base near Philadelphia, a city we both enjoyed. We picked Haddonfield, NJ, a charming small town across the Delaware River from Philadelphia. Haddonfield had nice homes, wonderful shops, and great restaurants. It was a perfect escape from military life and a great place to enjoy the area. Kathie and I had pooled our money before the wedding and put a down payment on a single-family house a few blocks from the center of town so we could walk to everything. It also afforded me the opportunity to carry her across the threshold of our house on our wedding night. The house was on a beautiful tree lined street and had a big back yard with tall trees and a picket fence.

As it turned out, I not only married Kathie, but also her golden retriever that she had named Crile. Crile was a great dog, but she loved to run away when she could. Our neighbors across the street had a high-spirited Irish setter named Murphy that liked to run away as well. Murphy's family solved the problem by leashing Murphy to two-gallon jugs of water when they put him out in the front yard. It was quite a picture to see Murphy pulling the water jugs down the block. Fortunately we did not have to do something like that for Crile because we had a fenced-in back yard. Or so we thought.

Our house in Haddonfield

We, of course, would walk Crile, but sometimes we just wanted to let her out in the yard to run around and not have to go out ourselves. This all worked fine for some time but something happened. One day we put Crile in the back yard and went into the living room in the front of the house only to see Crile flash past the window on her way down the street. We couldn't believe it was Crile, but a search of the yard came up empty. This began a search to find out how she had escaped. The fence was fine, but she had gotten out.

The next day we put her out again with the same result. The challenge was on. She would stay quite content when we were outside watching her, but the moment we turned our backs she was gone. We escalated our investigation.

I would watch from a window on the second floor of the house while Kathie put Crile out. She must have known that we were watching because she stayed until I came down the stairs and again saw here flash past the living room window. No matter what we did to hide, she somehow knew we were watching and would stay put. I thought that somehow she might be able to shinny under the fence, so I put wire between the pickets near the ground but this had no effect on securing her. Finally, one day as I watched from a parked car across the street, we discovered her secret. There was one set of pickets that were bowed in the middle. She would run at the fence, suck in her lungs, and dash right through the fence as though it was invisible. That was her last escape.

Cedarhurst NY: We moved from Haddonfield to Cedarhurst, NY in 1975 when I got a job with the FAA at Kennedy Airport. That is where we met our lifelong friends Liz and Jack, our upstairs neighbors. Liz was a primary school teacher and Jack worked for Mutual of Omaha. We soon discovered that Liz and Jack were wonderful and generous people who kept us laughing.

Liz's favorite comment was, "I don't exactly know what happened, but...." And then a wonderful story was told.

One of my favorite Liz stories was when she had a famous mobster's granddaughter in her class. The grand daughter had missed so much school that Liz went to the principal to see what she should do. Under NY state law if a child misses a certain number of days they must be sent back to repeat the year. The kid was within days of exceeding the maximum. This was early in the school year so it was clear that something needed to be done. The principal's advice was that Liz should deal with it. Liz made numerous calls to try to speak to the child's parents with no success. Finally Liz left a message telling the parents that she had no choice other than to send their daughter back if she missed any more days. This resulted in a meeting, but not what Liz expected.

It turned out that the child's older sister showed up to talk to Liz. Liz told her that she needed to talk to the parents. The sister said something like: " My folks don't talk to no teachers and my sister don't need no schooling. You need to pass her so that she can get through high school, then she is going to be married and be well taken care of." That night, Liz came home and told Jack the story and asked for his advice. He said, " I think you should start the car tomorrow morning."

Jack was a wonderful guy and great friend. He worked in Manhattan as a senior sales manager for Mutual of Omaha. His job was to finalize the deal with big corporate insurance accounts. That entailed entertaining various clients several nights a week. He knew every good restaurant in town and how to get around. One evening when the four of us were in NYC for a night out we met Jack at his office. He had dinner arranged at a great restaurant. Of course, the maitre'd knew Jack by name when he entered the restaurant and took us to a wonderful table. After dinner we went out to the street. Jack looked up and down then whistled and pointed at a black limousine. The limo stopped and the driver came over and opened the door. I couldn't believe that Jack had also arranged for a limo for us. He told me that he hadn't. Jack knew that limo drivers would look for fares while they were waiting for their clients to be ready to be picked up and knew just how to nab one for us.

Jack, Liz, Kathie and Me

There are lots of stories of our great times with Liz & Jack, but I'll tell one more. My Uncle Henry was a member of a very exclusive country club in Absecon, N.J. When he learned that I was stationed in N.J. he sponsored me for membership. We could not afford to go very often. It was, however, an incredible treat to be a member and go there, like experiencing the life of the wealthy in days gone by. It was rumored that the senior Kennedy's belonged. It was a place where you would pull up in your car and the bags and golf clubs disappeared. The bags would appear in your room with the clothes in the closets and shoes shined. The clubs would show up by the caddy master polished and ready to go. A small orchestra would play after dinner for dancing. Of course we had to invite Liz and Jack to spend a weekend with us there.

Walter, me and Jack

The club had two courses, a professional course and one for less experienced golfers. Jack and I were certainly going to try the easier course. The club required all golfers to use a caddy. Our caddy was named Walter. He handled both our bags and advised us on each shot. We were quite a challenge for Walter because our shots often went in different directions from the tee and not always on the fairway. It was, however, a wonderful day of golf and time together. As we approached the caddy shack we knew that we needed to treat Walter well for all his help. As Jack was my guest, I felt that I should give Walter a sizable tip for all his efforts helping the two of us. Unbeknownst to me, Jack felt he should tip Walter as my guest. It was not until we discussed the game over drinks in the bar that we realized that we had both generously tipped Walter. The next morning as we approached the caddy shack we heard a commotion. It was Walter pushing the other caddies out of the way jumping over the racks of golf clubs. He was shouting "they're mine…they're mine" pointing at us. Our golf weekend was not only a memorable experience for Jack and me, but for Walter as well.

Alexandria, VA: In June 1977, I was transferred to FAA HQ in Washington, D.C. Kathie and I moved into our newly renovated 1889 frame townhouse in Old Town Alexandria, VA. Our house was in the middle of 5 adjoined houses that were renovated by a builder R. I. Kellogg and Daughters. The architect had done a wonderful job of bringing light into ever room by putting a large skylight in the kitchen through the center of the house. The house was about 1,500 square feet with a living room – kitchen – dining room on the first floor and two bedrooms and bath on the second. The house was only 14 1/2 feet wide, but sat on a lot that was 125 feet deep that went halfway through the block. The view of our yard from the back of the house was like looking at a bowling alley (80 feet deep and 14 ½ feet wide),

but it was a perfect place for our dog Crile to run and Kathie to have a garden. Behind us was the Fannon Coal Yard with hug coal towers that were no longer in use but housed bats that would spectacularly fly out at dusk. We were in a great location, just a block and a half off of King Street where all the shops and restaurants were located. Our greatest surprise was that they built a subway stop that came within a few blocks of our house shortly after we moved in. This made commuting into DC very easy.

Kathie and I were the first to move into the newly renovated row of townhouses. We were about 11 blocks from the Potomac River yet our end of town had been overlooked by the city for years. When we went out house hunting for a place to live the realtor said, "I can not in good conscious show you a house west of Washington Street". We couldn't afford a house on the east side so we knew we were to become pioneers. When we first moved into our house there was a hole in the sidewalk in front of our house that had not yet been filled in from hooking up our sewer line. We had only been in our house for a couple of weeks when we experienced firsthand how run down our end of town really was.

The Rat: One night we woke up when Crile started barking at the kitchen sink. We couldn't understand what was happening until we went down in the kitchen. We could hear something rattling around in the trashcan under the sink and Crile wasn't happy about it. We soon realized that it must be a rat. There wasn't anything we could do in the middle of the night so we put a chair against the cabinet to keep it closed and brought Crile up to the bedroom. The next morning we called the exterminator. He told us that, yes it was a rat, and that it probably came in through the hole in the sidewalk. He could not be sure, however, if the rat had left the house or was still in the crawl space or walls. His solution was to bate the crawl space and under the sink but leave the hole in the sidewalk open. The plan was that the rat would eat the bait that would make it thirsty and it would go back to the sewer for water. When it drank, the poison would be activated and the rat would die outside the house. If it died inside the house, it would produce a terrible smell for a long time. We agreed to his plan and waited that night to see what we might hear. Again we heard the commotion under the sink.

The next morning was a Saturday, so I was off work. I went down to the basement to see if the bait had been eaten...it had. I was delighted until I heard a rustling behind me. It was the rat.

The rat looked at me. I looked at the rat. As I looked, it started to go into a spasm then right itself keeping its eyes on me. I could tell that it was under the influence of the poison, but was not sure that it wouldn't charge me. I slowly backed out of the basement to get fitted for battle.

It was summertime and I was in shorts. The rat had obviously not left the house and I didn't want it to die somewhere it was impossible to get to. I went up to the bedroom and put on a heavy pair of blue jeans and my Air Force combat boots. I am not exactly sure why, but I thought to put a small 22 pistol in my back pocket "just in case". As I returned to the basement I picked up a baseball bat to do battle. Our basement door was on the outside of the house. I needed to go down two steps outside and three steps inside to get to a small dug out area where I planned to have a workbench. This area was about a ten by ten foot area. Beyond that was a crawl space with about a five foot ceiling height four feet toward the front of the house then a dirt wall that led up to a two foot high crawl space under the remainder of the house. During the move I had put unpacked boxes on the first crawl space area for storage. That is where I saw the rat. When I returned the rat was nowhere to be seen. I cautiously climbed up into the lower crawl space and started to shake the boxes and probe between them with my baseball bat. My hope was to get another sighting and hit the rat with the bat. No, not here. No not there. All of a sudden the rat started to run up the dirt wall toward the narrow crawl space above. It was out of reach. Without thinking, I reached to my back pocket and with a circular motion over my head brought the muzzle down at the rat and fired. The rat flew up in the air, did a double back gainer, and landed at my feet. I hit it with the baseball bat and the battle was over.

Then I heard Kathie shrieking outside thinking that I had been shot. I emerged from the basement holding the rat by the tail and asked her to go get the camera. She took a great game hunter picture with my prey and my pistol in hand. That afternoon I put steel wool in the sidewalk hole.

We have never had a rat since. Perhaps the word is out on me. I would have put the picture here in this book for you to see except two weeks later our house was robbed taking both the gun and camera with the undeveloped film in it so you will simply have to believe that this is a true story or ask one of my friends.

Restoring our house: At first our block was populated with wonderful black families that welcomed us into their community. Some had lived there for generations nearing 100 years, but they soon sold out to developers and moved elsewhere. Over the 40 years that we lived there we saw the block turn over many times.

Some of the first neighbors to move onto the block were gay. We all became friends and took pride in fixing up our row of homes. We ended up replacing the front of our houses to restore them to the original 1890 German siding, dentals, and Victorian appearance from the colonial look provided by the builder.

Kathie and I had a carpenter named Barry who worked to restore our façade. A short vignette on Barry was that one morning just after he arrived he stuck his head in the door and said that his wife had called, he needed to leave immediately, and wasn't sure when he would be back. As it turned out he had bought an old stone house in Pennsylvania. They had been hearing noises in their attic above their bedroom and thought it was squirrels. Barry's wife was lying in bed that morning when the ceiling caved in dropping a family of six foot long black snakes into the bed on top of her. She had moved to a motel.

As it turned out the historian for the White House, William Seale, lived around the corner. He advised us all of the appropriate paint colors. He told us to put the siding color of one house as the door and window mullion color of another with a common trim color to tie all the houses together. All the neighbors agreed and we ended up have a uniquely wonderful row that was actually featured in the book <u>America's Painted Ladies</u>.

Cats: The next transition for the neighborhood was cat owners. Everyone had a cat except us (Kathie is allergic to cats). The most incredible cat owner on the block was Kay. Kay was an antiques dealer in her late 60s at the time, who lived in the attached house next door to us. She had a cat named Charles. She would let the cat out into the yard and then call for it by name.... Charles.... Charles. Of course, I thought she was calling me, so that took a while to sort out. Charles was a large black and gray Maine Koon Cat. Kay believed that Charles was the reincarnation of her grandfather. I will admit that Charles was extremely smart and had an authoritative air about him.

One time when Kay was on an antique buying trip she asked us to watch the cat for her. The next morning I was in our bathroom brushing my teeth and listening to the morning news on the radio. When I finished, I went next door to feed Charles before going to work. The following morning, as I was repeating my morning procedure in the bathroom, I heard a cat meowing. Our bathroom and Kay's adjoined each other. Charles had learned from the day before that after I brushed my teeth that he would be fed, and he was upset that it was taking me so long. Charles was screaming at the bathroom wall between our houses to encourage me to hurry up and feed him. That was repeated each day that Kay was away and stopped when she returned -- not to be repeated again.

Another time when Kay planned to be gone on a ten-day trip she asked another friend to house sit and watch Charles. After a week, the friend called us to say that he was leaving so we should look after Charles. After we agreed he told us that he hadn't seen Charles in a couple of days. He had let Charles out but he had not come home. We were distraught. We knew how much Charles meant to Kay and now we were either going to have to find him or tell Kay the bad news when she returned. And, Charles had a two-day head start on his adventure.

Kathie and I called the animal shelter, posted signs, drove up and down the streets around us calling Charles, no Charles. Finally Kathie got the idea to go to where Kay used to live by her antique shop. We drove there across US Route 1 and seven other city streets to Kay's old shop. Kathie opened the door and called for Charles. To our surprise, he came running up to her, jumped into her lap on the passenger side of the car, and put his front paws on the dashboard looking out the front window. It was clear to us that he was saying, "What took you so long. Take me home."

Kay & Kathie

Critters: Kay also had another cat named TJ. TJ was old and incontinent, so Kay kept him in the basement. Our houses didn't have a real basement as I described before. You had to go out into the yard and enter from a small door under the house. At Kay's house there was a small area that you could stand, but the rest was a crawl space that varied in height but was predominantly about two feet high comprised of dirt covered in 100 year-old dust. In Kay's mind a perfect place for TJ. Kay simply kept the small door to the outside open so TJ could go out or come in if it was cold or raining. She would also feed TJ in the basement. Unbeknownst to Kay this was not only great for TJ but also all the local wild life.

Sally lived in the adjoining house on the other side of Kay and was also in her late 60s. One night Sally came running over to our place shrieking that a huge animal was trashing her basement. As it turned out, Sally's house did have a half basement where she had her cloths washer and dryer and where she stored paint, garden supplies and equipment. She also used it as a bit of a pantry. We came running over to her place to find everything on the floor and back in the crawl space we spotted a huge possum.

Sally and Kay came over to our place to discuss what could be done. The possum had obviously come into Kay's basement through the open door and then to Sally's through a connection between the houses back in the crawl space. We called the City to ask what could be done and they offered to loan us a have-a-heart trap. They told Sally that they would loan it to her if she didn't get any blood in the trap. Sally agreed and, being a lawyer, took the admonition about blood seriously. That evening we set the trap in Kay's house near where she fed TJ and put several tasty morsels in the trap. Then we went upstairs, poured ourselves a glass of wine, and waited to hear the trap slam shut. About 30 minutes later we heard the bang and ran outside to the basement door.

YES! We had caught the biggest possum I have ever seen. I was delegated the opportunity to bring the cage and possum out of the basement. As I picked up the cage with the handle on its top, the cage rocked forward and the possum ran out. The cage had a defective latch and the possum was so large that the front gate opened when I lifted the cage. The possum, of course, did not run outside, but rather ran back to the front of the crawl space again.

The next morning I removed the cage and repaired the latch for a second attempt, hoping that the possum did not have a great memory. When we checked the trap the next morning we had been successful. I secured the openings with tape so that there would be no mistakes this time. That was probably not necessary because the possum had tried to get out and caught its lower pointy jaw in the wire mesh of the trap. Sally was delighted that we had caught the possum but went crazy when it was apparent that the possum's gum had bled in the trap. Kathie and I took the possum to a park by the river where we tried to release it. To my horror, I realized that the possum could not get out of the trap because its jaw had ratcheted four teeth worth into the mesh. So there I was trying to un-ratchet the possum while it flailed and hissed at me. I realized that I had bitten off more than I could chew so to speak. I worked at the possum's mouth with a stick trying not to get bit. Finally it was free and ran out of the trap. It ran about ten feet in front of me, then turned and gave me a dirty look, hissed, and ran away.

Possum and me after the release (Photo courtesy of Kathie.)

This was not Sally's only possum problem. About a year later she came running over to our house again yelling, "Get your gun". There was a possum on her fence hissing at her and she wanted it out of there. I told her that I wasn't going to shoot a possum in the city so she called the police. Next thing I knew two burly Alexandria police officers were standing in her yard looking at the possum guns at their side. They looked bewildered not knowing what to do. About that time, a second police car pulled up and a small black female police officer walked up to the others. "What seems to be the problem boys?" she said. They pointed at the possum and told her that they weren't sure what to do. She said, "Do you want him?". They looked at each other and said "NO". With that, she grabbed the possum by the tail and began swinging it over her head. By swinging the possum it couldn't turn to bite her. As she twirled it over her head she went back to her police car, popped the trunk, and threw the possum in slamming the lid down. She turned and said, " They're mighty fine eating" and drove off.

Possums were not Sally's only wildlife problems. The most memorable was when she was preparing for a dinner party at her house. The dining room table was set and she went back into the kitchen when she heard a strange noise from the dining room. She ran back into the dining room to find an owl perched on her table centerpiece. Sally was in the end house in our row and she had windows in the side of the house by her dining room table. She screamed and the bird flew back out the window. The owl must have liked Sally, however, because it had brought her a present. There in her bowl of beef bourguignon was a half eaten rat. Needless to say the dinner menu needed to be adjusted and Sally got screens for her windows.

While I am talking about Sally, I need to share her story about her 'whale flipper case'. Kathie and I have a great deal of respect for Sally. Her husband left her and her kids in mid life. Sally raised her kids and put herself through law school. When she moved in to our little row she was about 60 and an attorney for the Health and Human Services Department. Her specialty was defending the U.S. in lawsuits brought by Native Americans.

One of her cases was a medical suit brought by an Eskimo man. According to her story, many tribal people in Alaska love fermented whale flipper. Evidently, it is a real delicacy if it is prepared properly and sealed in casks for a stipulated period of time. Unfortunately, if it is not prepared properly it becomes a deadly poison. Because of this, the government has outlawed its preparation, making it a federal offense to prepare or eat it. That becomes a catch-22 for those who can't live without it. In this man's case, the man had eaten the delicacy and become ill. He went to the hospital where he knows that there is an antidote for the poison. However, if he tells the doctors that he has eaten the whale flipper, he will be arrested when he is cured. If he doesn't, then he can only hope that the doctors will give him the antidote before he dies. It was stories like this that made dining with Sally a fun time. I believe that the man in this case did survive the poison and jail.

Sally at her dining room table

I have one other Alexandria animal story worth telling. I had just had a wisdom tooth extracted and was lying on the couch when our friend Nancy knocked on the door with some soup she was kind enough to bring me. She was an incredibly thoughtful person and good friend. I was upstairs and I could hear her talking to Kathie. She said "Kathie, why do you have that rubber snake on you stoop?" Kathie told her that we didn't, so they opened the door again to look, and sure enough there was a five-foot-long black snake curled up on our front steps. Kathie called for me. Sore mouth or not, something had to be done. I told her that I would go get a shovel but she said "oh no...you can't kill it...I just want it out of here."

After some thought it came to me. I could go into our alley between the houses and get out our water hose and blast the snake with the spray. I hit the snake full blast and it slithered down the steps onto the sidewalk. I kept up the spraying moving it out into the street in front of the house and eventually across the street. To my astonishment, it climbed up the tree by the sidewalk and onto one of the large branches. Well, the snake was gone from our place, but it was still around. For several days afterward the neighbors would comment on the snake in the tree.

It was October and I assumed the snake was looking for a place to spend the winter. About three days after it had climbed into the tree, I came out of the house to go to work and the snake was gone from its perch. Then I saw it. There was a plumbing truck parked in front of the house across the street and I could see the tail of the snake hanging from the muffler of the truck. It was cold that morning and the snake found a warm spot to rest. I called to Kathie to come see. As she looked, the plumber came out of the house, got in his truck, and sped away. The snake was truly gone.

Dogs: The next transition for our neighborhood was dogs. Almost every neighbor had a dog. A neighbor in one of the new brick houses beside our group of frame houses had moved there from the country. He loved to hunt foxes. When he moved in he built a chain link pen in his yard to house his foxhounds. The pen was about six foot square and contained two large hound dogs that would bark at anything that moved in their sight. I felt really sorry for the dogs sitting in their pen night and day, in the heat and cold. I asked him why he didn't bring them into the house and his response was that that would ruin their ability to hunt. But this wasn't the only problem.

Every morning he would open the pen and let the dogs loose in the alley beside his house. The dogs were so excited to be free, they ran up the alley, turned left down the sidewalk and would come to the tree in front of our house to dump. He wasn't the kind of guy that was going to pick up after dogs, so we got stuck with the mess. I spoke to him about this and asked him to take the dogs to the nearby train yard to run his dogs, but he wouldn't listen. That called for drastic action on my part.

That weekend I went to a local hunting store and bought a small bottle of fox scent. Fox scent is used to train foxhounds and scare unwanted smaller animals away. That evening I went out into the alley and drizzled the fox scent down the alley, around the corner, and up the stairs in front of his house. I left a puddle of the scent on his doormat. The next morning he let the dogs out as usual, but with an incredibly funny result.

The dogs barked louder than ever as they rounded the corner onto the sidewalk. Then they ran up the six steps to his front door in a frenzy and dumped all over his doormat. He was livid...pulling the dogs off the stoop, stepping in what they had left behind, then dragging them back to their pen. The next morning the same scenario occurred. Kathie and I could hardly contain ourselves. After that he walked the dogs over to the train yard and our problem was solved.

The only other memorable dog story was a real surprise. The coal yard at the center of our block was transitioned into a parking lot. All the houses that face onto the surrounding streets have yards that back up to the parking lot. As a result, we can see all the backs of the houses around the entire block.

Someone had moved into a house around the corner with a dog that was kept in the yard during the day. The dog obviously wanted to be back in the house so it barked for hours to get in. After trying to live with this noise for some time, Kathie said that we needed to go speak to the owner to tell him our concerns. When the dog stopped barking, we knew the owner was home, so Kathie and I went over and knocked on the door. As the door opened I was surprised to see a large man in a sleeveless tee shirt wearing a shoulder holster and gun. I felt like running, but, I sheepishly said that we had come to complain about his dog. There was a moment of silence between us, as we looked each other in the eye. Kathie started to back away. Then he said, "I am so happy that you came to speak to me rather than call the city. I am an Alexandria Police Officer and if I was reported for making a nuisance I could be in trouble. I will take care of this and it will not happen again." The morals of this story are that things are not always what they seem, and when you have a problem with a neighbor, it is always best to speak directly to the person before taking other action. We never heard the dog barking again.

As I write this book our neighborhood has transitioned again. Now a new generation of neighbors is moving in and they all have babies. Old Town has been a great place to live and has been a great place to return to after work.

Chapter 5: FAA

In September of 1974, Kathie and I had just been married and were living in Haddonfield, NJ. My work as an Air Reserve Technician (ART) was not conducive to early-married life. It was almost impossible for us to plan anything when I could be called upon to fly to Europe or Asia if a reservist didn't show up for a flight. When I wasn't on a trip, I was one of four officers expected to monitor flight departures at all hours of the day and night. This was because our Wing Commander thought that the active duty personnel would blame the reservists if things went wrong and he wanted someone to be his eyes and ears. This meant that I would have to be at the base at midnight two nights a week in addition to my normal duty.

I had heard that the FAA was looking for pilots to become inspectors so I called for an appointment to speak to the Flight Standards Division Manager in the FAA Eastern Region Headquarters at Kennedy Airport in NY.

At the appointed time I went in and told the Director of my 3,000 hours of international flying time and how much I wanted to be an inspector. I was 28 years old. He told me how much he would like to hire me, but under the civil service rules I would be competing with retired airline pilots that had much more experience including 60,000 flight hours so it would be impossible to hire me into the civil service. Those were the magic words. I told him that I was already in the civil service, a GS-13 DOD Air Reserve Technician. He stood up in astonishment and said, "Can you start in two weeks?". He had been hoping to be able to hire younger inspectors. I said yes, signed the papers, and went to work for the FAA.

I left the ART position but retained my position in the Air Force Reserve unit. The next step was to move to Cedarhurst,

NY near Kennedy Airport where I would work after attending B-727 and inspector training at the FAA training center in Oklahoma City.

EASTERN 66: I believe that I was the youngest Air Carrier Operations Inspector in the FAA at that time. Most of the other inspectors in my office were in their 50s. On June 24, 1975 shortly after I returned from inspector training, Eastern Airlines flight 66 crashed on approach to Kennedy Airport. I had just come home from work when Kathie said that I needed to see the news. They were reporting that Flight 66, a B-727 had crashed on Rockaway Boulevard. That was my route home from the FAA office at Kennedy Airport. I had just missed being in the accident. It then dawned on me that I lived the closest to the crash and, as a newly trained FAA inspector and accident investigator, I should get to the scene of the accident as soon as possible.

I was one of the first on the scene and a grim scene it was. There was little left of the plane between the crash and the ensuing fire. The fire department had put out the fire and the police were in the process of sealing off the road. I showed my credential and went onto the site. The smell of the burned plane and 113 passengers was overpowering. We did not know it at the time, but the plane had been caught in wind shear. This accident was what focused aviation safety experts on the power of wind shear as a major flight hazard. My job at the scene was to observe and document the wreckage.

Other inspectors soon joined me from my office. We teamed up to compare notes as the night progressed. As I was discussing my observations with another inspector I looked up to see a microphone about two feet from my face. The press had arrived and one of the reporters had seen us talking. He had put his microphone under his armpit and backed into our conversation. In this way, we hardly noticed the microphone because the reporter was facing away from us and there were many people milling around working to remove bodies and secure the area. We, of course, were not allowed to speak to reporters so this was very upsetting. The next day it all became clear what the press was doing.

The National Transportation Safety Board (NTSB) was in charge of the investigation. They set up an office in a large room in a nearby hotel and began to interview those of us who had been on the scene the night before and to form accident investigation teams. I was assigned to the Weather Group. Each group had an NTSB lead, a representative of the Air Line Pilots Union, Boeing as the aircraft manufacturer, the FAA, and other technical experts as appropriate to the particular investigation group.

While I was waiting for my interview I wandered around the room and noticed Jules Bergman a well-known TV reporter at one end of the room with a camera in front of him. I wandered over to see what was going on. It seemed bizarre. He had a mike in his hand and was looking into the camera. From the angle you could see that the camera was filming him with the NTSB activities behind him. What seemed bizarre was that he would nod, shake his head, and change facial expression as though he was interviewing someone but there was no one there. Then I saw it. There was a tape recorder on the floor that he was listening to through an earphone. He was asking questions that had been developed around a tape that had been recorded previously, probably the night before at the accident scene. On TV that night, it looked like he was interviewing someone who didn't want to be identified at the NTSB investigation site, but there was no one there. Fortunately it wasn't me that he was pretending to interview.

Air Carrier Operations Inspector: I am delighted to say that my job was not filled with accident investigations. My primary job was to administer flight evaluations to airline crews in the simulator, conduct check rides so airline pilots could get their licenses, and fly enroute evaluations that consisted of riding in the cockpit jump-seat to evaluate the crew's performance in passenger service.

My first enroute was quite an experience. I was on my own for my first enroute evaluation. This was because it was considered double jeopardy for the airline crews to have more than one inspector on board, and because there was usually only one jump seat in the cockpit. Inspectors can only perform a check ride in aircraft in which they have an Airline Transport Type Rating (ATP). I only had an ATP in the B-727 from my FAA training at the time, so my first inspector duties focused on B-727 flight crews. The day before my first enroute, my Office Chief, Dick Klinert, called me into his office to give me some practical instruction. He knew that I had been a flight examiner in the Air Force and that Air Force flight checks were very detailed and rigorous. He told me not to expect the military discipline that I was used to and to not nitpick the captain. He suggested that I observe the flight and unless there was something egregious to simply thank the captain when it was over and come back for a debrief. Normally we would map out a flight itinerary in a circuit of flights with different crews that ended back at Kennedy Airport (JFK). My first was to be a flight on a flight to Chicago and back.

The next morning I showed up at the airline operations center at JFK to review the paperwork that the flight dispatcher had prepared for the captain. I went to the counter, showed my credential, and asked to see the paperwork and pick up my boarding pass. The dispatcher went into the back room and did not return for about 15 minutes. It was now about time for the aircraft to depart so I was getting nervous about being able to get to the plane before they closed the door. When the dispatcher returned he appeared nervous as well. Finally he showed me the paperwork and gave me the boarding pass. I raced to the gate and made it on board. The crew was waiting for me by the door to the aircraft. The flight was uneventful and I stayed onboard until returning to JFK. After landing I went to the FAA district office to meet with my Office Chief as he had requested. As I entered the office everyone started laughing, stood, and applauded. I looked at the Office Chief and he signaled me to come into his office. He asked me if I had detected any problems? I said no except for the length of time it took the dispatcher to respond to my requests. That is when he told me what really happened.

Evidently the dispatcher thought that I was an imposter. He had never seen an inspector that looked so young. When he went into the back room he looked on a list of FAA inspectors that they had on the wall for several years and my name wasn't on the list. With that, he called security and they had come to surround the dispatch office. Before they closed in the dispatcher thought to call the FAA district office to check and see if I really was an inspector. My Office Chief had answered the phone. The dispatcher told him that there was a kid impersonating an FAA inspector, obviously to get access to the aircraft, and he had a credential that looked very realistic. My Office Chief told me that his response was, " That is our new inspector, Charles Huettner, he is a real hard nose guy and you better not mess with him or he'll ground the plane." That is when the dispatcher nervously gave me the papers and the pass. The security police went away and I never saw them.

About six months later the Flight Standards Division Manager sent me to United Airlines training center in Denver for B-747 training. He told me that they thought it would be funny to have the youngest inspector checking the oldest airline captains and I was well qualified with my C-141 experience. When I received my Airline Transport License in the B-747 in July of 1976 I was the youngest 747 captain in the world (age 29). I say this because the oldest and most senior airline captains flew the 747. Now I was going to be giving them their flight evaluations for the FAA. This made for many stories. I will tell you one of the most memorable.

At my desk at the JFK Airport FAA District Office

My first 747 enroute was with Pan American Airways from JFK to Frankfurt, Germany. The 747 is normally used for long distance flights overseas because of the size of the plane. I went through the dispatch office as described above without a hitch. All the dispatchers knew me by then. I arrived at the aircraft early and introduced myself to the flight attendants as I boarded. It was a B-747-100 that had a spiral staircase to a top-level lounge and a door into the cockpit. As I entered the cockpit I met the flight engineer. Airliners had flight engineers in those days and I had to get a flight engineer license as well as a pilot type-rating license to do the inspections. I showed the engineer my credentials and then met the copilot who was setting up for the flight. I sat sidesaddle in the jump seat behind the captain's seat waiting for the captain to arrive. When the captain entered the cockpit I stood up blocking his path to his seat. I tried to make eye contact to introduce myself when he bent forward and started to get his approach plates and other flight documents out of his flight bag that he had put on the floor between us. When he stood up he put his hand on my shoulder and with one motion pushed me past him and out the door saying, " You have to go now sonny. I have to fly the plane."

As the cockpit door locked, I turned and saw the flight attendant, who was in the upper deck, dive down the spiral staircase to avoid any action I might take. Under federal law, it is illegal to interfere with an FAA inspector in the performance of his duty. Fines and license suspensions are possible. Of course I knew that the captain wasn't really to be blamed, but I wasn't sure how to handle this embarrassing situation given that I was going to spend the next eight hours peering over his shoulder during the flight.

After a pause during which time the other crewmembers informed the captain that I was an FAA inspector there to give him a check ride, the door to the cockpit crept open. The captain sheepishly said, "Um...Er...Welcome aboard". We got along famously after that.

ONA DC-10: As the youngest inspector in the office I was naturally the one they assigned to do the grunt work. I discovered that doing the grunt work well was the way to make a difference and get ahead.

One day the Office Chief called me into his office and told me that they were seeing too many bird strike maintenance problems at Kennedy Airport and that I should get on top of the issue. This required me to go around the airport to talk to the airline maintenance offices and search their information for anything that appeared to be related to bird activity. I carefully noted the time, date, runway involved and the extent of the damage.

Then I went to talk to the NY & NJ Port Authority representative who was responsible for a bird hazard prevention program. Their program consisted of a series of carbide cannons that would sound and supposedly scare away the birds. Kennedy's runways ran along Jamaica Bay not far from a city dump that also was on the Bay. As I conducted my investigation I noticed that the seagulls would pick up trash from the dump or clamshells from the beach and drop them on the runways to break open the shells for the prized meat. The birds would also congregate by the runways for warmth in cool weather. It was quite funny, if it were not so serious, to see the reaction of the birds when the carbide cannons went off. They would jump about 10 feet into the air and then settle back to their original position. I could see that something needed to be done to improve the Port's bird abatement program.

I produced a report after assembling all the maintenance information and observations and presented it to my office manager. In the report, I condemned the existing bird program and predicted that there could be an accident on a particular runway, time of day, and time of year if action wasn't taken. My office manager was surprised at the detail in my report and decided that he should take it to our Regional Director as soon as possible. As it turned out, the Regional Director had a scheduled meeting with the Port Authority leadership the next day so he planned to bring my report to the meeting.

Amazingly, the very next morning, a fully fueled ONA DC-10 sucked up birds as predicted in my report, lost two engines, and aborted the takeoff on the runway. The aircraft burst into flames and burned up as the fire department tried to extinguish the fire. Also amazingly, the 139 passengers all escaped without serious injury. This was because all the passengers were trained flight attendants who were prepositioning to the Middle East to service trips to Mecca for the Muslim Hajj. You can see the pictures at: (https://www.youtube.com/watch?v=1kiifVK92NA)

The dilemma for the FAA and Port Authority was that they had my report predicting this accident and didn't know if they should release it to show that they had identified the problems and were meeting to address the issues, or burry the report. They ended up doing a combination of the two. The report was not highlighted but the top brass at the FAA decided to take the issue seriously and establish a "National Bird Hazard Taskforce" to see what should be done at Kennedy and other airports around the country. They put me on the national taskforce and assigned me to monitor specific actions at Kennedy. My work on this national taskforce brought me to the attention of the Flight Standards Service Directors in Washington leading to my being promoted and assigned to FAA HQ.

FAA Regulatory Program: Kathie and I moved to Alexandria and I began to work at FAA HQ in 1977. I started out in the Project Development Branch of the Air Carrier Operations Division. My job was to create regulatory packages that would change the FAA regulations for airline operations. These packages consisted of "Rulemaking Actions" that would change the regulations for all operators and "Exemptions" to allow something different from what the regulation required for a particular operator. Exemptions require that the applicant prove an "Equivalent level of Safety" to what is required in the existing regulation.

Exemptions: We received numerous petitions for exemption from companies that wanted to do something different than what the rule required. I would review the request and based on my experience and others, I would draft an exemption or denial and take it to our legal counsel for review. After all the appropriate offices had given their concurrence by signing off on final paper it would go to the Flight Standards Service Director for signature. This was a much more streamlined process than is in place today.

One example of a petition for exemption that I worked on was a petition submitted by the Flying Funeral Brothers. The Flying Funeral Brothers were proposing to fly the dearly departed in small General Aviation aircraft strapped in as passengers rather than having the remains shipped in airline cargo compartments. This would be cheaper for the families, but rather bizarre.

The first question we needed to determine was if the dearly departed was a person or cargo. If the aircraft involved was a two seat aircraft then the deceased would be at the controls and need special tie-down requirements. We had to determine what the legal issue would be if the aircraft should be involved in an accident and one of the passengers was already dead. All of these and other issues were considered and special limitations needed to be addressed in writing an exemption for this unique operation.

Another petition was for an operator of a DC-3 aircraft. The petitioner wanted to outfit the aircraft with tanks filled with water to haul live lobsters from Maine to New York. For some reason the petitioner had not considered the fact that the water would flow to the aft of the aircraft during takeoff changing the center of gravity and flood the cargo compartment. In cases like these the petition was denied and the operator was spared spending a lot of money and an almost certain accident.

Rulemaking: Rulemaking is a much more complicated process. To make major changes we would develop a paper describing what we felted needed to be done and publish it in an Advanced Notice of Proposed Rulemaking in the Federal Register to solicit information from the community. After that we would draft and publish a Notice of Proposed Rulemaking (NPRM) stating what we proposed to do, why, how much the regulation would cost the industry, and open a comment period for responses. After the responses were reviewed, a final rule would be developed that would become a requirement at a future date allowing time for industry compliance. When I was working in the regulatory branch the Service Director could also sign off on the final rule. Later, the entire process needed review by the Secretary of Transportation, and now there is also a review by the White House Office of Management and Budget. As a result, FAA rulemaking has now become much more politicized than it once was. An example of a rulemaking action that I managed was changing the regulations for airline pilot training.

Simulator Program: In the late 1970s there was an Arab Oil Embargo and the price of aviation fuel skyrocketed. The airlines came to FAA to see if they could get a rules change that would reduce the amount of aircraft flying that they had to do for training. At that time, the airline training regulations allowed simulator training for all the required maneuvers and procedures except takeoff and landing and a maneuver called a V-1 cut. A V-1 cut was accomplished by accelerating the aircraft down the runway for takeoff. When the aircraft reached a speed at which it could no longer stop in the remaining runway (a calculated V-1 speed), the instructor would pull back an outboard engine on one side of the aircraft simulating an engine loss at a critical time. The student was expected to continue the takeoff, climb to 1000 feet, and initiate the engine failure checklist. Unfortunately some students didn't do well on this procedure resulting in some aircraft accidents and lost lives.

The airlines asked the FAA for permission to conduct all training in the simulator to avoid these maneuvers in the aircraft. I was assigned the project to see if this could be done while ensuring that pilots had the ability and experience to safely perform the maneuvers during an airline flight.

The first thing I needed to do was to see how the airline training simulators were programmed. What I discovered was that they did not have programming for ground effect. Ground effect is caused by a compression of the air under an aircraft wing when it gets close to the ground. If you have ever felt a plane float slightly above the runway before it touches down during a landing, you have experienced ground effect. Simulator manufacturers did not have flight data to computer model ground effect for a simulator so the simulated plane would simply land perfectly every time in the simulator. So here was the dilemma. How could I write a regulation that required something that didn't exist?

I began by talking to the airline engineering and training community, the airline pilots union, and the simulator manufacturers to see what could be negotiated. The airlines wanted us to simply allow the training in the existing simulators. The pilots union wanted the simulators programmed to accurately reflect ground effect and other hazardous conditions like wind shear. The simulator manufactures told me that they could probably get data from each type aircraft for landing from the aircraft certification data, however it would be expensive for the simulator manufacturers to buy this data from the aircraft manufacturers. It would also require the airlines to buy new simulators that had the motion and visual systems capable of accurately presenting ground effect to the pilots. I was facing the old "chicken and the egg" dilemma of needing an upgraded simulator to allow the training, yet no one knew if it could be built at a price airlines were willing to pay. Another hurdle was that the FAA rulemaking rules required that we include an economic impact statement showing that the rule was reasonable. I had no information about what this all would cost.

To gather more information I went out to the three groups of stakeholders (airlines, pilots, manufacturers) and asked them to provide me with the information I needed. They wouldn't respond. The airlines wouldn't tell us what they would pay, the manufacturers wouldn't tell us what creating the simulator might cost, and the pilots wanted everything without worry of cost.

I struggled for some time to see how I could get the information that I needed until my Ah Ha moment. By then I knew what each of the stakeholders didn't want the FAA to do so I created a proposal that incorporated everything that they didn't like. I privately called it an "Argumentative Draft Regulation". I sent it to each of the groups and waited for the reaction. It was swift and forceful, containing everything but the four letter words that were written between the lines. The good news was that they fought the proposal with detailed arguments that provided me with the information I needed to craft a reasonable rule.

After receiving their responses, I called them to personally tell them what I had done and thanked them for providing what I needed to create a draft that would be well received. The resulting "Notice of Proposed Rulemaking" was received without negative comment and in 1980 the "Advanced Simulator Regulations" and Appendix H to the airline Part 121 regulations were adopted.

Today airline pilots are trained in simulators that are capable of accurately simulating the entire environment around them including wind shear and other adverse weather conditions. This became a reality by creating a regulation that did not require any of the stakeholders to do anything. I wrote the regulation to simply say "If a simulator could achieve this------ then FAA would permit this training in it". Airlines could see an economic benefit of not needing to fly the aircraft so they pressed the manufacturers to develop simulators that the FAA would approve. We created a special team of FAA inspectors who would certify the simulators as we certify aircraft. A revolution in simulator development, airline training, and aviation safety was the result.

RBO: After my successful efforts in simulator training my Branch Chief, Cliff Weaver, retired. I was promoted into his position. After considerable time seeing the breadth of rulemaking petitions and exemptions it occurred to me that there was a better way to regulate airline operations.

The existing airline operating regulations are contained in 14 CFR Part 121. They are prescriptive regulations that required specific equipment and operating practices. Many of these regulations had been developed over the years in response to airline accidents. For example, they required a certain number of fire extinguishers based on the number of passenger seats in the aircraft. The thought was that the more seats, the bigger the plane and therefore more fire extinguishers should be available on the plane. My idea was to turn these prescriptive regulations into performance-based regulations that would require an airline to meet a safety objective not state how it must be met. Performance-based regulations would permit more possible solutions to the problems addressed and free the industry to be innovative as they had been for simulator training.

A performance-based regulation to replace the number of fire extinguishers would be to require "a means to extinguish any potential fire aboard the aircraft". My experience with the simulator regulation also suggested that we provide this approach as an alternative to the existing regulation. In this way an airline could choose to install the number of fire extinguishers required by the existing regulation OR devise a fire suppression system that might be more effective and possibly weight less thereby saving fuel and maintenance costs. This would require testing and FAA certification, but once shown to be effective, the course of aircraft design and flight operations would progress to be safer in the future. I called this approach "Regulation by Objective" (RBO).

I tasked one of my regulatory development branch members to start to rewrite Part 121 in the new format and went to my Division Manager, Dick Collie, and my Associate Administrator Walt Luffsey to get their approval to proceed. They in turn raised the idea to our Administrator, J. Lynn Helms. He liked the idea. While this was going on, I was talking to Roger Fleming of the Air Transport Association (ATA) to see if I could get the support of the airline industry. As it turned out Administrator Helms was scheduled to give an annual report to the House Transportation Committee. He testified before Congress regarding our interest in pursuing this approach to rulemaking. I was feeling great that we might begin a new era in aviation. My excitement was short lived.

The ATA lobbied Congress to stop the program. I used the experience I had from writing the simulator regulations to make the RBO regulations an alternative to the standard regulations so that no company was forced to change rules. My thought was that as companies developed better methods of achieving the safety goals in a way that would also save them money we could slowly move to the new approach. The industry, however, feared that FAA would see new approaches to current regulations as good ideas and then mandate them, raising operating costs. "Better to not come up with new good ideas if you have to live with them". The project was terminated. Later Roger Fleming came to me to say that he thought that the industry made a mistake in killing the program. They were too set in their ways to imagine a better way.

As I write this in 2016, I am delighted that the FAA has picked up on the idea of performance-based regulation in the creation of the new Unmanned Aerial Systems (UAS) (Civil Drones) certification and operating rules. Faced with so many different aircraft with so many different uses and operating capabilities, RBO is the only approach that will allow this new industry to grow while maintaining safety. I doubt that any of the people at the FAA today remember the RBO program from the 1980s, but those concepts are finally winning acceptance as the preferred regulatory method 30 years later. Imagine what would have been accomplished if those regulations had been in place that long.

Atlanta: Tom Imrich and I were identified as rising stars in the Flight Standards world, but neither of us had worked in a regional office. Associate Administrator, Walt Luffsey, spoke to both of us and told us that we needed regional office experience for our career progression. He contacted the Regional Directors in Seattle and Atlanta about bringing us in as Flight Standards Division Managers. Tom went to Seattle, and I went to Atlanta to work for Jonathan Howe the Southern Region, Regional Director. I enjoyed working in Washington so the plan was to spend a couple of years in Atlanta then return for a position at HQ. In January 1982, Kathie and I packed up our house in Alexandria, rented it because we expected to return, and the movers came to collect our worldly possessions. We decided to spend our last afternoon in the DC area by going to Clydes for lunch in Georgetown. That is when all hell broke loose.

We parked on the street near the restaurant. It was cold but beautiful out. Clydes is a cozy restaurant famous for their burgers. We sat in a leather-covered booth and had a leisurely lunch reminiscing about what we had experienced in Washington. As we emerged from the restaurant we were amazed to see that there was about an inch of snow on the ground and a lot of traffic. We went to the car and discovered that the very efficient parking police in Georgetown had given us a ticket for parking in a snow emergency route. There had been no snow when we parked the car. As we complained about this to each other we started the car and turned on the radio to try to find out why there was so much traffic. An Air Florida airliner had crashed on the 14th Street Bridge and there was a fire in the Metro. While I was reeling from the shock of the ticket, plane crash and fire, it hit me. I was now the Southern Region Flight Standards Division Manager and Air Florida was, as of that day, my responsibility.

We eventually made it back to our house. It was completely empty except for a sleeping bag, some plants, and our pet rabbit, Watson. We did not even have a phone. Everything had gone with the movers. We had planned to sleep on the floor and take off for Atlanta the next morning. I had to go to a pay phone to call the command center to tell them where I was and explain that I would be out of touch until I reached Atlanta. Yes, this was before cell phones and my only link to my bosses and staff in Atlanta was through a pay phone.

Kathie and I depart for Atlanta- January 1982

The roads were terrible as we made our way south. I was driving Kathie's Porsche 914 and she drove our Volvo wagon. Boy did it snow. As we drove down I-95, we had to travel in the ruts made by the eighteen-wheelers. We had a CB radio to talk to each other between cars and I could tell that Kathie was rightfully getting upset. Finally we saw an exit at McKenny, Virginia off I-85 south of Richmond and we pulled off the road. Fortunately, there was a motel right at the exit that had a room and we booked in for the night.

The next morning we loaded the plants and rabbit back into the car and headed south again. The snow had stopped and the interstate was cleared, but as we approached Atlanta the roads became a sheet of ice. They had experienced an ice storm while we were getting snow. Ice is worse than snow. Late that afternoon we arrived at our apartment at Post Lakes and unloaded the car. I slid down the icy sidewalk to a payphone by the apartment swimming pool to call the FAA Command Center to let everyone know I had arrived and find out what was happening. I didn't even have a TV to watch the news feeds. I spoke to Jonathan Howe my new boss and he filled me in on what was happening. It was over to me to guide FAA actions from then on.

The next day the moving van arrived to deliver our household goods. The driver came up to me after moving everything in to apologize. I asked him why? He said, "You gave me a hard time about my not wanting to take your unopened bag of charcoal, but I finally relented. You said it was no more burnable than the wood of your furniture and I finally agreed. Well, that really worked out well for me. I got stuck in the snowstorm and pulled off the road for the afternoon and night. When I went to start the truck the fuel had gotten so cold the truck wouldn't start. So, I lit your bag of charcoal under my fuel tank and got the engine started." I nearly died on the spot. He could have set the truck and everything in it on fire. It finally occurred to me that the moving company doesn't want to haul charcoal not because it is a hazardous material but because of its drivers. A driver and a bag of charcoal together are the hazard.

My experience with airline accidents from my Kennedy Airport days provided me with what I needed to do to support the NTSB and our inspectors during the Air Florida accident investigation. Our role really stepped up after the onsite investigation. It turned out that the pilots had not been trained in cold weather procedures so we launched a special investigation of Air Florida. I personally lead the FAA team because the VP of Operations at Air Florida was Dick Scully who had been the FAA Flight Standards Service Director prior to his retirement. He had been my ultimate boss when I first joined the FAA and would be a formidable opponent during the investigation.

At one point during the investigation Mr. Scully asked me to meet with him in his office. He told me that I was off the mark and was creating problems. I outlined our activities and said that I thought we needed to stay the course. He told me that I was wrong and that I should expect a call from the FAA Administrator to rein me in. About an hour later I was in the investigation office when the secretary informed me that I had a call from the Administrator. My heart began to race as I tried to think of how I should respond to him. I took up the phone and said, "Yes sir". He said, "Charlie, I just got a call from Dick Scully. He is really upset." "Yes sir", I said. You must really be getting close to their problems. Keep up the good work." I couldn't believe it. The FAA Administrator had called to congratulate me not chew me out.

This was a time in the FAA when professional expertise was recognized and rewarded despite political sensitivities. Selection into every professional position in the agency required a background of education, training and experience for the position. Promotions came from within the technical path. The Administrator was a fellow pilot and there was no one who would second-guess the FAA Administrator on aviation safety issues within a Presidential Administration. And, as demonstrated, the Administrator stood behind his employees.

Tom Imrich: I mentioned my friend Tom Imrich. While I was moving to Atlanta, Tom was moving to Seattle. Tom is the most brilliant person I have ever met. I am troubled that the FAA never fully recognized what a talent they had working for them; fortunately Boeing later did.

The Deck: Tom personally built a deck at his home in Virginia before his move and invited Kathie and me to see it and have dinner on the deck. This deck was fabulous. The base of the deck was at the back of the house over a significantly down-sloped backyard. It was about 10 feet in the air supported by 12 x12 beams that Tom had salvaged from the revamping of his family's 100 year-old farm barn back in Pennsylvania. It had two levels with benches built into the railings so he could have a huge crowd on the deck during a party.

I don't know what it is about being a guy, but his deck was so great I simply had to find something to rag him about. I found it immediately. As I stepped out of the sliding kitchen door onto the deck I had to step up. Everyone knows you should step down onto a deck. So I said, "Wow Tom, this is a great deck, too bad you didn't measure the height right". He said, "I didn't. You have to know what I measured the deck for." With that he told me that the reason he built the deck as he did was because of the gnats that bothered him when he went out onto his patio on the ground.

Besides being a pilot, Tom is an aeronautical engineer with a master's degree from MIT. His solution to the gnat problem was to capture a number of them and assess their aerodynamic characteristics. He then determined their typical "service ceiling" (how high they could possibly fly) and build the deck above it so that the gnats wouldn't be able to bother people on the deck. I told him that I had heard a lot of excuses for miss measuring before, but this was the best. He said that it wasn't an excuse and took me to his office where he had a notebook full of gnat specifications and deck drawings and calculations. I had to admit to how amazed I was and congratulate him on not only a great deck, but also an amazing aeronautical success.

The Moving Fiasco: Tom bought a new car when he was about to move to Seattle so that the mid winter cross-country trip would be a safe and pleasant one for his family. It didn't turn out that way.

The first problem on the trip was the passing of their beloved pet canary Tweetsy. Tweetsy did not survive the nearly freezing temperatures, while stranded for hours on a remote stretch of Interstate highway in mid-winter Wyoming where their car broke down. The breakdown was due to a massive engine failure on a brand new Olds station wagon. Tom's kids were very upset, at Tweetsy's loss and conducted a funeral along the road.

After being towed to Salt Lake City the next morning, the Olds dealer mechanic told him that the car was too new for them to have the required parts in stock, so they would have to spend a day or two until the parts arrived. Tom immediately called the movers to tell them that he couldn't make the original delivery date for his household goods. They told him not to rush and told him to call them when he arrived in Seattle. Finally the parts came in, the car was fixed, and Tom and family arrived at their new home.

When Tom called the movers he got the REALLY BAD news. The van carrying all of their worldly goods had been involved in an accident and many of their possessions had been scattered across the highway, damaged, or destroyed. Welcome to your new home in Seattle.

Landing on the Golf Course: My last story involving Tom was years later when Kathie and I went out to visit Tom and his family on vacation. Tom had called another friend Joe who formerly worked for FAA, and then worked for Boeing, and arranged for the three couples to fly in Joe's airplane to dinner (Joe was a partner in the airplane along with several other of his Boeing colleagues).

Joyce, Joe, Kathie, Tom, & Dee before the flight

The plan was to fly to the San Juan Islands for dinner. The day arrived and we met Joe at the airport. All three of us are pilots so we did a thorough preflight and got into the six-seat, single-engine, Cessna Centurion for the trip. Joe was in the left seat as pilot in command. I was in the right seat to work the radios and Tom and Kathie sat behind us in the middle seats. The other two wives sat in the back seats. We did the engine run-ups at the end of the runway, got tower clearance, and took off.

We climbed to 1,500 feet and only went about 10 miles when the engine began to run rough. Joe tried adjusting the fuel mixture, but the engine began to sputter worse. Finally, Joe switched to the alternate fuel tank thinking that perhaps we had some bad fuel when the engine stopped. As I looked out, all I could see were houses, buildings, water, and trees. Not a great place to land.

Joe was aiming to ditch in Lake Washington, near the shore. Fortunately Tom had already been looking for an emergency landing "field" after the first plug on the first cylinder had misfired. He said, "Its OK Joe, we are over a golf course.... right under us, ...there's your spot". Sure enough, directly below us was the Overlake golf course. We did a spiraling 270-degree turn to line up with the 13th fairway heading from the green to the tee. As we set up for a final approach we could see we'd have difficulty clearing a church and power-lines in our path. It was at this point that I experienced one of the most tender moments in my marriage. Kathie reached forward and took my left hand.

We briefly traded some airspeed for a reduced sink rate, to miss the church and power-lines, while Tom reached forward and told Joe that he was also pulling the prop control back into "high pitch" (to reduce drag), to help extend the glide. To further extend the glide we needed, we elected to wait until we passed the power-lines to put the landing gear down. But when we finally selected "gear down" we had less than normal hydraulic pressure due to the engine failure. As a result, the gear was slow to extend, and only the nose gear locked down. As we hit the first mogul of the fairway the nose gear of the plane sheared off, but the plane stayed straight on course. I was feeling all was in control until we approached the second rise. At that point, I thought we might flip over because the nose was heading down as the terrain was rising. Fortunately the prop hit first and kept the nose up. We softly settled into the grass and slid to a stop without any injuries. Just as we stopped, the right wing tilted to the ground and fuel started to drain from the right tip vent. There was silence for a second... all thankful for a safe landing... but then Tom's wife Dee (a former flight attendant for Allegheny and US Air) saw the dripping fuel and from the back seat loudly "commanded"... "Release your seat belts and leave the Aircraft"!

The exit door was beside me but I was the last to exit the plane. Along the way I had dropped the microphone and it had wrapped itself twice around my leg, trapping me. I finally extricated myself from the plane and noticed a battalion of golf carts descending on us. We motioned them away because of the fuel leak. They just kept playing, right around the downed airplane, complaining that they had a tournament the next day and there was no way that we would be able to replace the divot we made in the course. It was at this time that Joe realized that he was a member of the club and thought of the assessment. Then the fire department and police showed up. They advised us not to leave the area until the FAA had arrived.

Airplane after the flight

Well, Tom was the FAA Deputy Flight Standards Division Manager for the Region at the time, and I was from FAA

Headquarters, ...so the FAA had already technically arrived! However, we didn't want the headlines to be: *FAA Crashes Plane on Golf Course*, so we told the police that we would comply with their request. We discussed what we should do and agreed that Tom should go to the clubhouse to call the FAA region, and in-turn district office duty officer, to have them process the needed event notification and send out an inspector. He also asked the office to inform the inspector they were sending to treat the event professionally, and not obviously "socially recognize" the people who were in the plane.

While Tom was doing that, the Club Manager spoke to us saying that the Eyewitness News helicopters wanted to land and interview us. We definitely didn't want that to happen so we convinced him that the FAA would not like the press involved, that there would be liability issues if he let them land, and that we would not speak to the press. He denied their request.

We had suffered a rare and improbable dual magneto failure that isn't supposed to happen. Normally both magnetos are in use at the same time, and provide redundancy. But it turned out these magneto's (mags) were individually failing internally while enroute, after being in service for many flight hours. The failures only occurred when the mag reached high operating temperatures. It wasn't until the same failure occurred in both mags, that the engine would stop. FAA eventually issued an Airworthiness Directive regarding the maintenance inspection times and modifications to these mags to correct the failure issue.

The night of the accident we ended up eating pizza at Tom's house watching ourselves on the 10:00 news. Not exactly the evening we had planned.

Sothern Region Flight Standards Division Manager: After my ordeal moving into our apartment, reporting to duty at the

Southern Regional Office, and dealing with the Air Florida initial responses, I had the opportunity to meet my staff and began to visit the 15 District Offices under my Division. I was responsible for all the inspectors in the southeastern US including Puerto Rico and the Caribbean. My regional office was in a building across the highway from Atlanta Hartsfield Airport. The district offices were in NC, SC, GA, FL, AL, MI, TN, KY, Puerto Rico and the Virgin Islands. In Washington the issues I dealt with were technical and policy issues. In the regional office the issues were primarily personnel and budget issues.

I visited each of the offices and learned about their problems and opportunities. In time, deep budget cuts required that I close several offices causing concern for how to minimize the affect on my employee's lives. I decided to keep people in place where I could to avoid them having to move. They became home-based satellite offices reporting to the District Offices that I was able to afford. I celebrated many retirements and was fortunate that in the end we took care of everyone and had no grievances.

Personnel issues were the hardest part of the job. One day, one of the secretaries in my office asked if she could speak to me about her career. I agreed and she came to my office to talk. She wanted to become an inspector. I explained that she would need to get a pilot's license and experience and we began to discuss a plan for her to accomplish her goal. She then turned to me and said, "I would do anything to become an inspector". I explained the process again. She said again, "I mean that I would do ANYTHING to become an inspector". Then it hit me what she was saying and I realized that I was alone in my office with her. I immediately ran to bring my secretary into the room to witness the conclusion of our discussion. It became apparent to me that I needed to be very careful not to be put into a position that would compromise myself. It was episodes like this that caused me to yearn to be back in Washington dealing with aviation safety issues instead of personnel and personality issues.

Trip from Hell: Part of my job was to speak at various industry events. I was invited to speak at the Helicopter Association International national meeting in Miami Beach, Florida. What a debacle. There is a government rate for travel on official business. The allowance for hotels and food is not generous and unless a hotel offers a government rate equal to what is allowed it can be hard to find an affordable room. In the case of the helicopter meeting, the convention hotel cost a lot more then I was allowed to spend, so I looked at their literature for alternative hotels. I found one not too far away and made my reservation.

My flight landed at Miami airport and I went to the car rental to pick up a car. They gave me the documentation and keys and told me to get on the van outside the office to be driven to my car. I handed the driver my paperwork and sat down. The van loaded up and began driving around the airport dropping off various passengers. After quite some time, I was the only person left on the van and it kept driving. Finally, we pulled up into a lot at the far end of the facility. The driver told me that I had been given an upgrade to a Lincoln Town Car. He dropped me off by the car, handed me my suitcase and my keys, and drove away. Then I saw it.

I was at a black Lincoln Town Car, but my heart sank when I discovered that the back window was shattered, the seats were ripped, and the radio was missing. To make matters worse, the car wouldn't start so I was stranded in a nearly vacant parking lot about a mile from the rental building. I had about three hours to get to the opening reception to meet my host. Of course there were no cell phones in those days, so I was stranded until someone in a car drove into the lot. I begged them to drive me to the rental office. They finally gave me another car and I made the van driver stay with me until I checked it out.

Now time was ticking away so I drove as quickly as I could to my hotel. It was in Miami Beach. The hotel turned out to be a tall white stucco building that appeared to be a bit run down. I don't have the greatest sense of smell, but that didn't stop me from being almost knocked over as I entered the lobby. As I approached the front desk, I saw about 30 elderly people in wheel chairs parked around me. The guy at the front desk asked me what I wanted. I told him that I had a reservation. He looked surprised, but found my reservation and asked me to sign at the bottom. I told him that I wanted to see the room first. He asked his assistant to take me to the room. We went up a shaky elevator to the sixth floor and down a dark and dirty hallway to a room on the right. As he opened the door I could see a double bed with no headboard, a sink, a small dresser, and a chair. By this point it was clear that this was a residence hotel / assisted living facility for the underprivileged that rented out unused rooms to anyone who would stay. I didn't.

So now, I didn't have a room, the reception was to start in 30 minutes and I was a sweaty mess physically and mentally. This was clearly the trip from Hell. I drove back across the causeway to Miami from Miami Beach stopped at the first decent motel I passed and checked in government rate or not. When I finally arrived at the reception, I asked the association leader how they selected my original hotel to include it on their list of alternatives. He admitted that it was selected by its proximity to the conference hotel, but no one had checked it out. I gave him my report.

Balloon Celebration: The first un-tethered human flight in a hot air balloon occurred in France on November 21, 1783. My Regional Director, Jonathan Howe, decided that we should celebrate the 200th anniversary of this ground breaking event by launching a hot air balloon flight from the FAA regional headquarters parking lot on November 21, 1983. The idea was to highlight aviation and its history in the Press through our great celebration.

We lined up an instructor balloon pilot and asked him to be in our parking lot at 7:30 AM. The plan was to take off from the parking lot and head toward Stone Mountain Park a few miles from our office. Jonathan wanted one of us to ride in the balloon and I was selected because I am a pilot and was the head of the Flight Standards organization.

I arrived early on the day of the flight to meet the pilot, check out the preparations and discuss how we would proceed with the flight. I had never flown in a hot air balloon before. As a precaution, I put a walkie-talkie that connected me to the Southern Region Command Center in my pocket in case anything went wrong. As launch time approached my pilot launched a helium balloon to see which way the wind was blowing. All seemed to be going well, so the pilot and his wife started to inflate the balloon.

I climbed into the gondola and our pilot gave it the gas. It was actually a large flame of propane that went up into the balloon with a great whooshing sound. Slowly the balloon lifted us about a foot off of the ground to great applause from those attending. The pilot signaled his wife who was to drive their truck to Stone Mountain to meet us when we landed. More flame and the balloon began to rise higher. It was very exciting for all to see. Then the unexpected happened.

As we rose above the headquarters building the balloon began to change directions and drift across the superhighway I-85 towards the airport not toward Stone Mountain. We found ourselves on a collision path with the Atlanta Hartsfield Tower during the morning rush. When the pilot saw what was happening he handed me his radio and said, "you better call them".

I was flabbergasted. We couldn't descend without hitting oncoming cars and it looked like we couldn't continue without hitting the tower. I tried to call the tower on his radio, but got no response. I discovered that my pilot didn't have the tower frequency. All of this was happening at light speed. Then I remembered my walkie-talkie. I called the Command Center, told them of our peril, and asked them for the right tower frequency, Finally, I connected with the tower and told them that we were in the balloon that was racing toward them. They said, "Go back". I told them that we couldn't. They said, "climb" and we poured on the flame. We were approaching the tower at a 90-degree angle to the runways. The tower was located about half way down the parallel runways and between them. Our engine roared and we started a steep ascent. I was delighted to see that we were climbing above the tower elevation.

At this point my instructor pilot was laughing saying that he couldn't believe what was happening, and saying over and over, "The ballooning club will never believe this". I didn't see any humor. I saw my career and my life flashing by. As we floated about 300 feet above the tower the wind shifted and we started to track out between the two parallel runways. My relief at not hitting the tower was short lived. Now a more ominous fate awaited us.

As I looked out I could see two lines of airliners turning onto final approach for each parallel runway. On the left was a line of planes turning right onto final. On the right was a line of planes turning left onto final. We were in the middle at about 750 feet in the air. From our vantage point the aircraft were landing below us on both sides, but we were tracking out against the traffic flow. At this point we decided to not climb or descend for fear that our track would change and we would cross into one of the airline traffic flows.

At one point, as we tracked outbound we were at the same altitude of the landing aircraft. We could see the passengers with their faces against the windows staring at us. We could hear the approaching aircraft call into the tower to report a hot air balloon in front of them. By now the tower controllers realized that the balloon had been launched by the FAA, so they coolly replied, " Yes, this is our celebration of the 200th anniversary of manned flight, you are cleared to land Runway 27 Left." Under FAA regulations a balloon has priority over fixed wing aircraft in flight due to the lack of ability to steer the balloon. What this means is that if we were to drift toward one of the oncoming lines of aircraft, the controllers would have to break the aircraft off and send them around for another approach. This would disrupt the airline schedules, cost more fuel burn, and result in multiple lawsuits against the government. I prayed that we would maintain a steady track. We did.

We finally drifted beyond where the airliners were approaching the airport. With the aircraft behind us, we began a descent. There appeared to be a large field with a large building at one end that would be a perfect place to land. The pilot tried to contact his wife on the CB radio he had, but we were so far in the opposite direction from Stone Mountain that there was no way we could reach her. That meant that we needed to land somewhere that there was a phone to call her at a prearranged number.

As we descended toward the field we saw a large number of men run into the field. We came down within about 100 feet and called out to them to ask permission to land. They waved their arms and gestured, but would not answer our request. We went a little lower in the hope of being able to hear them better then we saw what was happening.

I know that this is hard to believe, but it turned out that we were trying to land in a monastery and the monks had a vow of silence so they couldn't give us permission to land. The pilot remembered that he had been to the monastery and bought bread from the monks some years earlier. So we gave the balloon the gas and headed further to look for a landing spot.

We floated over a marshy area, then spied a farmhouse with a large field in front. We came down to within 20 feet of the ground and blasted our jets to attract some attention. We got it. The farmer and his family all streamed out of the house. We asked if we could land and they agreed. With that we opened a vent in the balloon and settled onto the ground. The balloon collapsed and dragged us a bit tilting the gondola and we emerged.

What an experience. Our pilot went into the farmhouse to call his wife and we all helped him fold up the balloon. It then sunk in to me that I was responsible for enforcing FAA regulations and I was sure that the pilot had violated many of them. I also didn't know what the ramifications of our flight had been with the airlines and the Press. I told the pilot that we needed to get back to the tower as soon as possible to face the music.

As we parked in the Tower parking lot I told the pilot to wait in the car while I went up to see the Tower manager. As I reached the manager's office the door was open and about ten controllers were assembled to greet me. They were silent and stone faced. There was a pregnant silence. Then everyone in the room except me began to laugh. They knew how upset and embarrassed I was and began to reassure me. The local Air Transport Association office had called to launch a complaint, but since no adverse effects had resulted everyone backed off. The press had not made an issue of it either, so we were off the hook. That was the last hot air balloon flight sponsored by the FAA Regional Office.

Trip to South America: One of the responsibilities of the FAA Southern Region was to be an aviation technical ambassador to the countries around the Caribbean. We had a King Air 200 aircraft that we would use to fly to our facilities around the region. On one occasion, our Regional Director arranged for a trip to Colombia, Venezuela, and Ecuador to help aviation officials improve aviation safety and service for US air operations into their countries. Included on the trip were the Southern Region Division Managers of Air Traffic, Airways Facilities and myself representing Flight Standards.

When we arrived in Colombia we were met by two young men and a woman who were part of the "young Turks" who were taking over high-ranking positions in the country from their parents. They were very friendly, interested in talking about new aviation facilities they needed to purchase from the US, and anxious to discuss how the FAA could be of assistance to their efforts moving forward. They drove us to an estate in the middle of a coffee plantation that looked like it was right out of Heidelberg, Germany. It appears that many of the wealthy families had come to Colombia from Germany after WW II. We spent an enjoyable evening talking about aviation and their lives in Colombia.

Our next stop was Venezuela. After some official meetings, we were invited to dinner at the home of the man who headed Venezuela's Aero-Club. We were told to arrive at 5:30. We drove and parked at a large house in a block of houses in the Capitol. From the street, the house appeared to be like the other houses on the block, but as we were ushered into the front door it was apparent that the street façade was only one room deep opening again onto a large courtyard with wings of the house on each side. There was a railing and cliff at the rear of the yard. The cliff dropped several hundred feet to the valley below. The courtyard was beautifully manicured. Waiters in short white jackets presented us with drinks and we met our host. What followed was the most remarkable dinner I have ever had.

Our host walked us around the courtyard discussing his passion for flying. As we stepped up to the railing at the cliff's edge he asked us to look further out. The view below revealed a corporate airport at some distance from his house. There was a runway directly in front of his house running parallel to the cliff. On the far side of the runway was an aircraft hanger. Our host pointed out that the hanger doors were open to show us his private jet.

As we talked further other people began to arrive. I met his son who told me that his family had the air-conditioning franchise for the country. Obviously they were well off. While we talked, waiters delivered an incredible dinner. It started with canopies and drinks. Then small plates with meat, fish, potato, vegetables, and salad all in bite-sized pieces were served so you could continue to stand and talk while eating a gourmet dinner. By the time the dinner was complete and they were serving the dessert, the courtyard was filled with people. At one point our host introduced me to the Vice President of Venezuela and several high ranking military generals.

Finally, people started to drift away and it was time for us to say our goodbyes. I can remember thinking how vulnerable the attendees of the party were to be in a city neighborhood with all these dignitaries. My view changed as we departed the house. There was a military tank at both ends of the street and a hundred or so soldiers stationed along the street. This was certainly unexpected. They had quietly moved all this military protection into position while we were having hors d'oeuvres and dinner. Obviously, this was not like the diplomatic parties I have attended in Washington DC.

Our final stop was Quito, Ecuador. Quito is one of the cities with the highest elevation in the world, over 13,000 feet. It was a challenge to our King Air but we made it. It was like being on the top of the world. We saw a city there that looked like the Spanish and Inca's had built it long ago. After our discussions we flew back to Atlanta to follow up on the action items resulting from the trip.

Harvard: In 1984, The FAA sponsored me to attend a one-year mid-career program at Harvard's J. F. Kennedy School of Government for me to take courses toward a Masters Degree in Public Administration. Kathie and I moved into the third floor of a frame row house apartment (bay windows and all) owned by Harvard housing that was located behind the Divinity School in Sommerville. If you ever get the chance to attend classes at Harvard do it. It was a most remarkable experience.

The program started in August with a review of everything you needed to know from High School and College. In one month I took classes in speed-reading, succinct writing, and an incredible mathematics course that started with addition and ended with Calculus. The once-a-day math course went so quickly and succinctly that I actually understood how all the individual math courses I had taken years before all came together. We also reviewed the basics of statistics and economics. I have to say that if High Schools or Colleges routinely taught a similar course our country would have a much smarter and capable electorate.

Each of my professors was great.
- Robert Reich's (Later Labor Secretary) course taught me how important human capital really is. Companies that close plants and move for cost reasons often don't factor in the cost of losing a facility full people who know what they are doing, a huge mistake.
- My negotiation course from Roger Porter taught me that I should try to get what I value by offering something the other person values more than I do. If that doesn't work expand the negotiations until it does.
- My course on Presidential Power from Richard Neustadt showed me that the President cannot really command much of anything. His or her power comes from 1. What he says (Bully Pulpit), 2. What he focuses his time on, 3. What he signs, and 4. Who he hires. The latter three are a test of what the President says. I believe that this is true for more than Presidents.
- Professor Richard Light showed me how important statistics are to making good decisions.
- Howard Raiffa taught a great economics course. The basis of the science of economics stems from people and companies operating in their own self-interest. There is lots of this going on these days.

The final professor I will mention is Ron Heifetz. His course on "Leadership Without Authority" was the greatest course I ever took. Ron graduated from Harvard Medical School as a surgeon and psychiatrist. He is an accomplished cellist. He later graduated from the Kennedy School and has taught there ever since. The question behind the course was how to be a leader when you do not have authority. Most courses of this type focus on being the head of an organization. This course assumed that you weren't.

There I was, the first day of class in a room of about 90 students sitting at desks that formed a four-tier semicircle around a stage at the bottom center. Professor Heifetz came into the room at the appointed time for class and stood in the center of the stage. He began to look around the room and we all anxiously waited to hear what he had to say. He didn't say anything. He continued to look around the room. After about five minutes the class began to fidget. After fifteen minutes everyone was looking around restlessly. After 20 minutes someone yelled out, "So what do you have to say?". More silence.

After a half an hour someone spoke up and started to question him. At this point he said, "What have we just experienced here?" The point was made that someone from the group had lead the group toward something that we could all learn as opposed to learning something from the leader / professor. This was the first step in our learning how to move a group forward without commanding it. The trick to it, as Professor Heifetz showed us, is to ask questions, feel the energy in the group, and not stress the group to the point where it will kill you off figuratively or literally if you move the group forward at a pace that they can't stand. Ron's amazing combination of skills and insights have influenced me ever since.

Back at FAA: After my year at Harvard it was time to return to FAA headquarters in Washington D.C. My reception at FAA was unexpected. Rather than embracing the fact that I had returned with new insights and skills, I was practically shunned. FAA is primarily a blue-collar organization so the assumption was that all this Harvard stuff had gone to my head in more ways than one. I think "Mr. Smarty-pants" was the term some used. I was humbled by the opportunity and ready to bring some new thoughts to the management team. Fortunately, shortly after my return Allan McArtor became the FAA Administrator.

When Allan was appointed Administrator, there was only one year until the next Presidential election so he had to act fast if he was to make a difference. He created an initiative called "Impact 88" because he only had 1988 until he would probably be moved aside by the next administration. He created a team from senior FAA officials across the technical disciplines that were not in key positions. I was fortunate to be one of them.

We were directed to identify 8 objectives that we might achieve within the year and told to do whatever we needed to do to accomplish them. It was a fabulous opportunity to have the Administrator's support and free rein to make a difference. While we didn't accomplish all eight objectives in the year, we had them far enough along that the next Administrator, Admiral Jim Busey, followed through with most of them.

One of the accomplishments of Allan McArtor was to create the Office of Aviation Safety under a new Associate Administrator. This organization was to work across the other FAA lines of business to ensure that aviation safety was not compromised by problems between individual FAA organizations. For example, the Airports organization would work to improve safety at airports, but they did not necessarily coordinate with the Air Traffic organization or the Flight Standards organizations that focused on airlines and general aviation operations. Allan selected Keith Potts, who was heading the ATC organization as the new Aviation Safety Associate Administrator and me as his Deputy coming from Flight Standards.

We went to work assembling experts from each line of business into a small force that represented aviation and FAA as a whole. We would get the members of our organization together and discuss issues and connections between organizations, do some research to identify problems, and then meet with the program offices to discuss our findings. This was not well received by the program offices.

As we struggled to become an effective organization, Keith was diagnosed with prostate cancer. His focus on his job helped him hold on during a many-month struggle. I ended up helping him stay as involved as possible while running the office day to day. We came up with a concept called a System Safety and Efficiency Review (SSER). The idea was to pick a major airport and form a team of technical experts from all disciplines whose job was to observe what was going on at that airport and develop a report identifying exemplary activities and opportunities for improvement. This was not received well by the program offices either.

One example of an attempt to improve safety by our office was over the issue of infant child restraints. Our office did an analysis that showed that the only things on an airline aircraft that were not tied down during takeoff and landing were children under the age of two. Restraining children is not only important during an aircraft accident, but also during turbulence. A twenty-pound baby immediately weighs 60 pounds in a 3G-turbulence bump and is impossible for a parent to restrain. Airline seats are stressed for 9Gs to prevent them from becoming detached during an accident. That would put the infant at 180 pounds. Putting infants in the same seatbelt as a parent would result in the parent crushing the infant. We went into the accident database to see how many infants were injured during turbulence or accidents and discovered that the age of the injured is not recorded so we had no way to provide definitive data, however the risks are self evident. So, we recommended that infants be restrained in a child safety seat as they are in automobiles.

I took our analysis and recommendations to the Associate Administrator for Aviation Standards, Tony Broderick. He told me that he would not take action. I, therefore, appealed to Administrator. This resulted in an Administrator's Management Team meeting in the FAA Round Room (so named for the huge round table around which all the Associate Administrators sat for staff meetings and major actions).

On the day of the meeting Administrator Busey asked me to present my case. When I finished, it was Tony Broderick's turn. Tony admitted that we were not restraining infants, however to do so would mean more parents would have to buy a seat for their infant that was not currently required. He went on to say that this would mean that more people would drive to their destination rather than fly because of the cost. Since driving is more dangerous than flying, the risk to infants would be greater if we required them to be restrained in aircraft than if we didn't. In my rebuttal, I noted that FAA's responsibility is aviation safety and that we should fulfill our mission without worrying about other ways infants could be injured. There was dead silence in the room. Finally the Administrator spoke and said, " You make a good point Charlie, however, if I don't stand behind the person I have selected to run our regulatory program then I should fire him, and I don't want to fire him". In other words, I lost the argument and it was clear that I would lose any future disagreement with the leader of a program office. Our office was no longer able to be effective. What makes matters worse is that the regulations are still unchanged 30 years later.

Chapter 6: B&B

Kathie and I moved back to Alexandria from Harvard in 1985. We had rented our house while we were in Atlanta and Massachusetts. We thought that renting it to a single woman would be a good thing because a woman renter would be neat, clean, and take good care of our house. This shows you how bad stereotyping can be. We have had bad luck with renters. The first renter was a professional woman who was delightful and paid her rent on time. Then one day I received a call from her. She asked if there were any restrictions about her having a baby in our house? I said no. She then told me that she was getting older and it was now or never to have a child. She said she didn't know anyone she wanted to marry, but she was looking for someone who might contribute well to her gene pool, but if she was successful she wanted to know if that would be OK in terms of her lease. About ten months later her baby was born. She stayed on for a while then got a job outside the area and asked if she could break the lease. I agreed. She said the she was grateful, so she would try to find me another renter. Unfortunately she did.

I didn't hear much from our next single woman renter until it was time for us to come back to Alexandria from school in Boston. As the time for us to move back came closer, she stopped paying the rent. Fortunately, she did move out in time for our return, but what a mess. The house had been trashed. Candle marks up the walls, pet stains on the carpets, and I don't want to speak about the bathrooms. What made matters worse was that she declared bankruptcy. Kathie and I went down to the court to read her file and discovered how lucky we were. She had run up thousands of dollars on many credit cards, had a bad car loan, had borrowed money from all her friends, and only owed us two months rent. The letters in her file from her friends were heartbreaking. They were tearful letters talking about what a close friendship they thought they had with her, and how they couldn't understand how she could do this to them. The good news for us was that she had moved out. If she had not, by law she could have stayed in our place until all the legal actions were completed and that could have taken a long time. We were able to move back in so I could begin my work back at FAA as described before.

After some time back in our house, we realized how small it was and looked for a way to add just one more room. Living in an 1889 house has its limitations about building up from a structural standpoint. Our next-door neighbor at that time was a 20-something single guy who was a stockbroker named Bill. Bill was a real charmer and was doing well until the junk bond market tanked and he needed to sell the house. Unfortunately for him his idea of home ownership was that any money you put into the house was a waste. Just buy, hold, and sell high.

One day about a year before things went bad for him, I noticed there was some siding on the back of the house that was loose and sticking out. I suggested he get it fixed right away before the rain came in. I was concerned for him <u>and</u> us because our houses are attached. He declined. When he finally realized that he needed to sell the house he called in a realtor to begin the sale process. She told him that the house was unsellable. The entire back of the house was spongy. You could push on the rear windows and the frames would push in and out. In the basement the water had flooded so many times from the rear wall that the bottom of the water heater had rusted. When I went into his basement there was about four inches of warm water, obviously leaking from the hot water heater. In the end, we decided to make a deal with Bill to buy the house, half out of self-defense and half to get more room for ourselves. We had to put $35,000 into repairing the house to bring it to the point where it was saleable and a bank would give us a mortgage to buy it. That left us with two mortgages, one on 216 and a refinanced mortgage on 218. We needed some additional income to make this all work on a government salary.

Charlie Goes to Court: We hit upon the idea that we could open a Bed-and-Breakfast (B&B). That would give us more room for family and friends visiting us, and income to pay the second mortgage. But further renovating of the house, meeting all the zoning requirements, and obtaining a special-use-permit to open the business would take time. So, against our better judgment, we decided to rent the house until we could get everything we needed for the B&B in place.

We ended up renting it to a woman attorney who worked for the Justice Department. We had advertised the house at the going rate, but reduced it by $500 per month believing her sob story that she was just getting started on her career and needed a break. We agreed to the reduced rent if she would take a 6-month lease. At that point we planed that the rent would go to the original figure or we would begin our B&B. Sixty days prior to her lease being up we advised her of the new rent and asked her if she wanted to sign a new lease. That is when things got ugly. She told us in no uncertain terms that she would not renew her lease. It was unfair for us to raise the rent on her and she would be looking for a new rental. I asked her to put that in writing and I wrote her a letter terminating her lease at the original termination date. I thought everything was concluded with our renter, so I ordered new windows for the house, lined up a contractor to restore the front of the house, and purchased our business license. About a month later she came knocking on our door with a bottle of wine and told us that she had changed her mind. Obviously she had discovered that what we were asking for rent was very reasonable given the house and location. However, by then we were committed to moving forward with the B&B so we had to tell her that it was not possible for her to stay.

As the date arrived for her to move a check came through the mail slot with a note advising us that she would not move. I wrote back and told her that she was in violation of the lease and that she must move. By the end of that month she was still in the house, the windows had arrived at the distributor and we couldn't wait any longer.

We went to the small claims court in town and started eviction procedures. We received a court date and she filed for an extension. About two weeks later we received a registered mail package containing her argument to the court as to why she should not be evicted. Not being a lawyer, I found this to be most remarkable -- that she would tell the court and me her side of the argument before going to court. The following week Kathie and I arrived at the courthouse at the appropriate time. We sat on the left side of the room our renter sat on the right with several of her Justice Department lawyer friends. When the judge called our case she jumped up and said, "Your honor, I filed for a summary judgment of this case." What I didn't realize is that a summary judgment means that both sides submit their arguments in writing and the judge rules without coming to court. Not knowing this, I had filed nothing so I would have lost if the judge had agreed to hear the case out of court. Fortunately he didn't. His response to her outburst was, "This is your day in court." He then turned to me and said, "You may call your first witness." It was then when I realized that I should have had a lawyer. I was participating in a game where I didn't know the rules. I had no choice but to proceed.

"I call myself your honor. Here is a copy of the lease, here is the note where she told us she would not stay, here is the note giving her the 60 day notice required by the lease, here is her rejection, here are the contracts that I signed banking on her leaving. I request, your honor, that you help me remove her from my house so that I can begin my restoration and open my B&B." The judge turned to her for a response. She presented copies of the front of several checks that she had given me after the lease had expired and told the judge that my acceptance of the checks showed an implied lease and therefore she should not be evicted. He turned to me and asked if this was true. I told the judge that I had accepted the checks, but on the reverse side where I needed to endorse the checks I had written on each one "This is not accepted as rent, but will be held in escrow until she leaves the property". I then presented the actual checks to the judge for him to see for himself. Her actions proved to the judge that she was using her knowledge of the law to take advantage of me and he was not happy. He turned to her and said, "Tender the Property". She had been humiliated in front of her fellow attorneys. She jumped up and ran out of the courtroom. The judge then said, " Bailiff, bring her back here". With that, the guy with the gun ran after her. She was brought before the judge where he told her that she had a right to appeal within 30 days. That was the end of our day in court.

The next day Kathie called the court clerk to see if she had filed an appeal. She had not, but the clerk told us that we would be notified if she did. The clerk then said, "You know your renter is really nasty. She came in here like we are a bunch of flunkies ripping us up for not getting her the summary judgment she asked for. I'll tell you what. If she isn't out of your house at the end of the 30 days on the dot, I will be very happy to have the Sheriff throw her things on the sidewalk." She did not appeal and did move out. However, that is not the end of the story.

About two weeks after our court date we were talking to our friend Dianne who lived on the other side of the B&B. She told us that she had decided to rent her place and that our renter had just signed a contract with her. Our ex-renter was to be our neighbor! We didn't want to spread ill words about our renter to the people around us so we had not told Dianne about the problems we had just experienced. Our discussion came too late for Dianne. Dianne also found out that it was not easy to get our renter out of her house either when the lease with her was up, but Dianne had the advantage of knowing what game was being played.

Herb Kaiser: One good thing about living in Alexandria is that we are not too far away from friends that I flew the C-141 with at McGuire. One of my pilot friends, Herb Kaiser, lives in Rumson, NJ, not far from New York City, I have to tell his story.

One day Herb and his wife Jan drove their new car to NYC, parked in a parking garage, and went to the theatre to see a show. As it turned out when they got to the theater, the attendant told them that their tickets were for the following week. Herb and Jan discussed going out for dinner, but because they would be coming back the following week they decided to just go back home.

They went back to the parking garage and asked for their car. The garage was not busy, but they waited and waited for their car. Finally Herb smelled a rat and told Jan to go get a policeman. When the police showed up they demanded to go to the car. When they arrived on the upper floor of the garage, they were shocked to find that there was a winch hanging over the car. Thieves in the parking lot were in the middle of removing the engine from their car. They were swapping out the new car's engine with an old one so that the theft wouldn't be discovered until the replacement engine broke down. Herb and the police were amazed. The police said that it is somewhat common to find thieves swapping out tires and batteries in parking grarages, but they had never seen someone switching out an engine before.

We Start the B&B: Finally the house was ours again, the construction was completed and we were ready to open the B&B. The last step in the process was to file our business license with the court. I was at work at the FAA so Kathie took the paperwork down to the courthouse to file the documents. The staff looked over the papers and said to Kathie, " Is this a corporation, partnership, or sole proprietorship?" She said, " I don't know, I guess a partnership". The clerk then said that they couldn't process the paperwork unless both partners were there to sign the documents. Kathie then said, "Well, then make it a sole proprietorship." and signed the paperwork. The B&B was now her business.

Kathie has done an OUTSTANDING job of creating a beautiful and comfortable B&B. Unlike most B&Bs travelers get the entire 1890 townhouse for themselves; for 1 to 5 people traveling together. Her statement on her website says: "My objective is to give you the feeling of the happiest travel experience you have ever had." and she has achieved that objective for over 20 years. It has been a joy to us to meet so many interesting people and hear so many touching stories.

We had a family from Germany come to stay for several days. The Son flew in from the west coast where he was working, and his fiancé and parents flew in from Germany. The son spoke fluent English, the fiancé some English and the parents almost none. We invited them to come have a glass of wine with us on their first night to see if we could help them get around. We asked them what they wanted to see. At the top of their list was the Holocaust Museum. We were a bit surprised by this, but we told them how to get there on the Metro and invited them back the next night to see what their impressions were. The next night as we sipped another glass of wine they began to tell us about a wonderful thing that had just happened.

They went to the Holocaust Museum and took the tour. It starts at the top of the building and winds it way down telling the story and showing graphically the horrors that happened. They told us they thought the tour through the museum told a story that was fare and balanced, but it was the bookstore that made a lasting impression.

As they were looking through the books they found one that described a battle between the Allies and the German regiment that the Father had served in. The Father began to cry. He had been drafted in the army, outfitted, put on a train, and had fought in the war. He told us through his son as interpreter that he didn't know where he was. All he knew was that he had fought, many died, and his regiment had been defeated. He had lived the rest of his life in shame for the war and his unit's defeat. Then he found this book in the bookstore. It described the campaign that he fought in; told the entire story that had never been printed in Germany. Then came the clincher. The book said that the German's fought valiantly. Valiantly! Here was his adversary saying that he and his unit had fought valiantly. There is honor in defeat if you fight a valiant fight. His life of shame was over. We all toasted him and he smiled.

Charles & Darlene: While we have met hundreds of people through the B&B, some people become friends and some become lifelong friends. Charles and Darlene are two. Charles called us many years ago to book a reservation for his son – it was to take his new bride on their honeymoon. They turned out to be a lovely young couple that we really enjoyed talking to. We invited them over to see if we could help with anything and they told us their story.

The son said that growing up he thought that his father, Charles, was rather odd. He would go to the drive-in-bank and the teller would say "Thank you Mr. Smith". The son would ask why they said this because their name wasn't Smith. The son had noticed other odd things until one day he was watching the news and saw his father knocking in a door with the letters FBI on his back. His father was the Station Manager of the FBI office in Miami.

After Charles heard the glowing report from his son about their stay at our B&B, Charles called us to get a reservation for himself, his wife Darlene, and another couple. We had a great time talking to them and they later came back to stay again. Soon we were invited to Charles' home near Ashville, NC. We enjoyed the mountains and the simple country fairs with them. When Charles retired from the FBI he began giving Christian family counseling sessions.

Charles, Darlene, and Me

Fast forward several years and Charles called me to tell me that his daughter was selected to go to the FBI Academy and wanted to know if the family could come to stay. By then we had become good friends and we were delighted to see the entire family again. We were invited to tour the Academy and attend the graduation ceremony where the new agents receive their credentials. Fast forward again and now we are invited to Charles' daughter's wedding to another FBI agent. We knew we were safe at the reception when 30 FBI agents were celebrating with us. We now have two generations of life long friends from a simple reservation at the B&B.

Paul and Glenda: Another life long set of friends came to us as B&B guests. Paul and Glenda came from San Antonio, TX to stay while Paul was on business. He worked as a senior executive at USAA Insurance Company. When I heard this I was excited to talk to him because USAA is our insurance company. As they sat in our living room I asked him to carefully look around. I told him that I wanted him to be a witness for me if I ever needed to file a claim. We really enjoyed their company and were delighted when they called to come back to stay again.

On their second visit they asked if they could bring their son along. We said sure. When we had time to visit on that trip Paul said his son was coming to DC to test the waters to see if Governor George Bush might have a chance for a Presidential run. His son worked for Governor Bush and was one of his advance men. To make a long story short, Governor Bush won the Presidency as I am sure that you know, and Paul's son and his son's girl friend (later wife) both ended up in the Presidential Advance Office planning the logistics of Presidential trips and appearances.

I was working in the White House at the same time and became close to them. It was wonderful to get to become like family to these two outstanding young people from the next generation. We have subsequently traveled with Paul and Glenda and one day they invited us to come to their ranch.

Paul's family has owned a ranch near the Arizona / Mexico border for several generations. He and Glenda invited us to come down along with our very good friends Susan and Charlie Walker who live in Tucson.

Charlie is an astronaut that flew three space shuttle flights in the 1980s. He was the first commercial astronaut flying scientific missions for McDonnell Douglas. Easter 2012, Charlie was interviewed for the Smithsonian Channel in our B&B when they were filming stories about the space shuttle Discovery. He has lots of great stories to tell.

From Susan and Charlie's house in Tucson it was a trip of several hours south that ended at a dirt road. We were told by Paul to call him on our cell phone when we begin driving down the dirt road because we would soon be out of cell phone range and he new we should arrive at the ranch 45 minutes from the time we called. So we called and started down the road. As we drove, we started seeing signs telling us not to pick up any hitchhikers and to watch out for bears. As we approached the ranch we drove across a stream that crossed the road and found the steel gate open. We drove up to the old ranch house and parked.

The ranch house was from the 1800s and looked it from the outside. Inside it looked like Ralph Lauren had decorated it. Incredibly cozy with a large screened porch and a large table for dining. What we didn't realize at first was that the stove is a wood-burning stove, there is no electricity except when you started the generator, and the only wire coming to the house is a phone line so that they can communicate.

Paul & Glenda at the ranch

There is a large meadow that spreads out from the ranch house with trees all around. While much of this part of Arizona is desert, Paul's ranch has a stream running through it that waters trees that are quite tall and beautiful. A short distance from the main house was a bunkhouse that Paul built for guests. It is a new building, but looks quite old because they have used old wood and corrugated steel sheets, as they would have in the 1800's. Glenda is a wonderful decorator and cook. She and Paul gave us an incredible dinner under kerosene lanterns on the porch. The next day was wonderful. The ranch was an experience I will never forget. The views, sunsets, food, and discussion were unmatched.

216 B&B has been a wonderful addition to our lives. We have been able to pay the bills for the house, make wonderful friends, grow our extended family, and experience many things that would not otherwise have been possible. While Kathie managed the B&B, I continued to work at FAA. In 1995 FAA Administrator David Henson passed over selecting me to head the Safety Office so after 8 years of running the office as Deputy I looked for another opportunity. By that time I realized that enforcing regulations wasn't the path to improved aviation safety it is research and improved technology. I decided that it was more important to do something important than to be important. I looked to NASA.

Chapter 7: NASA

In early 1995 my career took a turn as a result of changes at FAA and a Washington AeroClub Luncheon. The AeroClub is an organization with members from all segments of the aerospace community in Washington DC. Members includes DC representatives of all the major aerospace companies, airlines, airports, industry associations, lobbyists, consultants, and congressional aides. They have a luncheon each month at a DC hotel that features a guest speaker. There are routinely several hundred people in attendance.

One month, I was unexpectedly asked to sit at the head table with the dignitaries. As it turned out, two FAA Administrators were also at the table, one seated on my left, was the Administrator that ruled against me on infant child restraint issue, and one on my right who had just decided not to select me to run the Safety Office. As part of the agenda, the current Administrator was presenting the preceding Administrator with his official portrait that was to hang in the FAA building.

As the luncheon program began, the President of the Club, Frank Jensen, amazingly, introduced me first. He asked me to stand up behind the head table, told those at the luncheon of my many successes for aviation safety, called me Mr. FAA Safety, and asked for a round of applause. This was somewhat embarrassing to the FAA Administrators and made me feel conflicted because I was getting great recognition by the aviation community yet I needed a new job. It was certainly nice of Frank to do this for me. And then a miracle occurred.

As we left the luncheon, I ran into the Associate Administrator for Aeronautics at NASA, Bob Whitehead, and asked him if we could talk. The result was my leaving FAA to go to NASA on a detail from FAA as the Director of Aviation Safety Research at NASA.

I loved working at NASA. The people were bright, dedicated, and professional. They saw me as an asset not a threat. NASA didn't have a research program focusing on aviation safety at that time. I was given free rein to visit the NASA Aeronautics Centers at Langley, Ames, Glenn, and Dryden (now Armstrong) and to interview researchers about existing programs that could be helpful to solve aviation safety problems. The researchers pulled out all the stops to show me what they were working on because my report could help to increase their project's budget.

An example of how research in one area could help aviation safety was an engine study at NASA Glenn. In this study, researchers were trying to identify engine fan blade problems. To do this they discovered a way to imbed tiny microphones in the engine casing. With multiple microphones they could use triangulation to identify a blade problem while the blades were spinning. Their objective was to improve engine design. I was very excited to see this because engine failure is an important cause of aircraft accidents. The current process for preventing engine failure was to remove the engine from the aircraft at certain time intervals, tear the engine down, and look for problems. This is very expensive and only detects a problem at that moment or when the engine fails. I asked, " What if you could put the microphones on all engines? Wouldn't you be able to identify a problem before it causes a catastrophic failure? Couldn't we move to a health monitoring maintenance system avoiding unnecessary engine teardowns and aircraft accidents?" The answer was yes, and today many new aircraft have engine health monitoring systems.

As you may have realized by now, my life has been filled with amazing "coincidences". I was about to have another one. As I was finishing my safety research report, TWA 800 crashed off the coast of Long Island, NY on June 17, 1996. A few months before, a ValueJet aircraft caught fire due to burning oxygen canisters and crashed. The White House responded by creating the White House Commission on Aviation Safety and Security Chaired by Vice President Gore. The commission later became known as the Gore Commission.

NASA detailed me to the Commission staff to focus on aviation safety. It was a thrill to be part of this extraordinary effort. The initial focus was on security. People thought that the TWA 747 had been shot down. The investigation later showed that the cause was a faulty fuel pump in the center wing fuel tank that caused a spark in the near empty tank. The tank exploded tearing the aircraft apart. But this commission wasn't an accident investigation like I had been involved with years before. The commission was charged with identifying ways to improve the nation's aviation safety and security.

As the former Deputy Associate Administrator for Aviation Safety and the Director of NASA's Aviation Safety Research Program, I was in a perfect position to merge some of my insights into the drafting of the Commission report. There is an old adage that whoever creates the first draft of a report has a strong influence on the outcome. I was the principal drafter of the safety portion of the report so I could merge ideas that came from testimony before the Commission with insights I have gained from 20 years of experience as a pilot and safety expert.

One of my inserts into the draft was to include a safety goal of "reducing the number of fatal airline accidents by 80 percent within ten years and 90 percent within 25 years". Many people thought that was crazy because the accident rate was already so low, it seemed to be impossible to achieve. Fortunately, the Vice President liked the idea and it became the battle cry after the President signed the report. But, that isn't the end of the story.

After the signing ceremony for the report, George Washington University hosted a dinner for the senior participants of the Commission and other dignitaries. Dan Golden, the NASA

Administrator, was seated next to Elaine Kaymark from the Vice President's office. During the dinner Elaine turned to Dan and said, "Well Dan, what are you going to do to achieve the Vice President's safety goal?" Dan said, "I'm going to invest $500 million dollars into safety research."

The next day I got a call from Bob Whitehead. He told me that he had just met with the Administrator who had said, "Don't you have someone from FAA who has been working on a safety research program? Well, I just promised the Vice President that I would put $500M into the program. Come back and brief me when you have the program laid out." I couldn't believe my ears. I believe that I am the first person in NASA history to have funding for a program of that size without having a program. I had to get busy turning a report and years of experience into a program that would provide the greatest safety gain for the dollar. We called the effort ASIST.

The first step was to assemble the best minds from the four primary NASA Aeronautics Centers, Langley, Ames, Glenn, and Dryden. Each of these Centers sent their top up-and-coming aviation researchers to help define a NASA Aviation Safety Research Program (AvSP). We decided to hold a series of workshops with industry to agree on a set of the most important accident causes and hear their thoughts about what would be most beneficial to eliminate them.

To meet the national goal of reducing the fatal aircraft accident rates, the NASA Aviation Safety Program focused on three areas recommended by a national team of more than 100 government and industry organizations: Accident Prevention, Accident Mitigation, and Aviation System Monitoring and Modeling.

The NASA Aviation Safety Program ended up working on eight technology strategies:

Make every flight the equivalent of clear-day operations.
- Bring intelligent weather decision-making tools, including worldwide real-time moving map displays, to every cockpit
- Eliminate severe turbulence as an aviation hazard
- Continuously track, diagnose and restore the health of on-board systems, leading to self-healing and "refuse to crash" aircraft
- Improve human/machine integration in design, operations and maintenance
- Monitor and assess all data from every flight for both known and unknown issues
- Increase survivability when accidents do occur
- Anticipate and prepare for future issues as the aviation system evolves

Major strides have been accomplished in each of the focus areas of the program, and the 80% safety goal has been achieved. The NASA leaders of the ASIST effort all became leaders of NASA Aeronautics organizations as well. Mike Lewis from NASA Langley ended up leading the AvSP and subsequently works for Boeing. Tom Edwards leads aeronautics at Ames Research Center and Jaiwon Shin who represented Glenn Research Center in the ASIST effort subsequently became the Associate Administrator of Aeronautics.

Following the success of the NASA AvSP it was critical to bring NASA and FAA together so that NASA technology would be implemented in the aviation system regulated and operated by FAA. I was able to establish a coordinating committee comprised of senior officials from both agencies that would be responsible for a smooth flow of research into operations. This led to a formal agreement between the agencies. The agreement restructured the existing coordinating committee into a new "FAA/NASA Executive Committee", and chartered it to oversee the success of the partnership to achieve the research goals. One significant change resulting from this newly established joint committee was that one council representing the diverse interests of the two agencies at the executive level would be responsible for harmonizing the civil aviation research and implementation efforts of the government.

Vice President Gore: One of the joys of working for the Gore Commission was working with the other talented staff members, Commissioners, and industry leaders who participated including the Vice President. I remember one of the issues we struggled with was how to reduce the General Aviation (GA) accident rate. Smaller GA aircraft have rather simple systems and are sometimes flown by inexperienced pilots. As a result, the GA accident rate is quite high in relation to professionally flown higher performance aircraft. The AvSP was looking for technologies to help pilots fly safer, however improved technology can be unaffordable for GA aircraft owners or unsuitable for their aircraft due to size, weight, and power requirements. So one of the big questions was how to help GA aircraft owners use improved technology?

I was able to discuss this dilemma with VP Gore. Without hesitation, he responded that we needed to get the technology we were developing into automobiles. "If we could do that, then the economies of scale would make it much easier and cheaper to put the technology in small airplanes. We might also be able to improve automobile safety." As it turns out, 15 years later the transfer of technology from aircraft to car and vice versa is all the rage in both industries. GA aircraft owners now can afford to have the latest GPS, glass cockpit displays, ground proximity warning systems, and other instrumentation that was unheard of a few years ago and we all know now of the efforts to develop driverless cars.

A funny story about the VP that I was told by one of his staff resulted from a car trip as they returned from a meeting. It is hard to believe today, but in 1999 people didn't have cell phones.

As a result, if you needed to make a call along the road you needed to stop and find a pay phone. On a trip the VP was making back to DC, the driver stopped at a pay phone along the road and the VP got out of the back seat to make a call. The staffer in the front passenger seat had her window down and was talking to the other staffer in the back. The call went on for some extended time to the point where the staffer in the front said "I wish he would get his fat ass back in the car so we can get back to the office". When the VP returned to the car he said to the woman, "Do you really think I have a fat ass?" Evidently, there was no glass in the phone booth so he could hear all that was going on in the car while talking on the pay phone. She, of course, was mortified.

Chapter 8: White House

In 1999 I got a call from the Office of Science and Technology Policy (OSTP) in the Executive Office of the President. They knew me from my work on the Gore Commission and follow-up activities. They told me that I was obviously the link and most knowledgeable of aviation activities between agencies. They asked me if I would be willing to be detailed to OSTP to become the Aviation Policy Advisor for the National Science and Technology Council (NSTC). I jumped at the opportunity.

It was a tremendous thrill to be working at the White House. My office was on the fourth floor of the "Old Executive Office Building" now renamed the Eisenhower Executive Office Building (EEOB). While the EEOB is not directly attached to the West Wing of the White House there is just a driveway between the buildings and both are located within the same secured area so I could walk freely from one building to the other.

The EEOB is a beautiful building with lots of history. The building was completed in the 1888 and was designed to be unburnable. In August 1814, the British burned the White House. When Congress authorized building the EEOB they stipulated that it not be able to be burned. As a result the only wood in the building are the handrails and office doors. Everything else is either stone or metal. The crown moldings are cast iron. The floors are marble in a white and black checkerboard pattern. The black marble has fossils in it. The doorknobs are cast brass with the shield of the Army, Navy, or State Department on them depending on the side of the building you are looking. Each of these departments owned one of the four sides of the building with the White House owning the fourth side. This was the entire federal government at the time. Boy, have things grown since then.

Kathie & Me in the White House

To get to work, I would take the Blue Line Metro to the Farragut West stop then walk down 17th street to the EEOB. I had a special badge that I would hold against a sensor then walk through gates and a metal detector to enter the building. My office was actually a cubical third one in from the hallway. It was about 4 feet by 5 feet in size, with a panel in front of me and a window behind that looked out on the roof. I was in the Technology section of OSTP.

OSTP is an amazing organization. It is headed by the President's Science Advisor and has political appointees that head the Science Division and the Technology Division. These Divisions contain civil servants detailed from various federal agencies that have significant science or technology missions. I was the aviation advisor detailed from FAA / NASA. The guy across from me was the space advisor. In front of me was the advisor for automobile and other transportation agencies. There were about 35 advisors like myself covering fields from healthcare to food safety. As the aviation advisor, I connected with the FAA, NASA, DOD, DOC, and DOA (yes, the Department of Agriculture has the largest fleet of aircraft after the DOD) etc. The President's Science Advisor could call a staff meeting and bring together representatives that covered the entire federal government.

An interesting sideline of OSTP history is what happened during the Nixon Administration. Evidently President Nixon and his Science Advisor disagreed over an issue to the point where the President told his Science Advisor that he didn't want to speak with him again. Nixon also didn't want to fire him for political reasons. During Watergate, the congress, knowing that there was a person on the Presidents immediate staff that did not support the President, subpoenaed the Science Advisor to testify. The White House cited Executive Privilege and would not let him testify. In response the Congress passed legislation that the President's Science Advisor would also be the Director of the new OSTP federal agency and appropriated funds for OSTP. As the head of a federal agency the new Director would be required to testify before Congress thereby negating Executive Privilege for future Science Advisors.

I came to the WH under the Bill Clinton administration. When I first arrived, I was told that every email that I received or sent would be recorded, stored, and become part of the Presidential Library files for future study. This was the perfect excuse for me to write all my friends that send me email garbage to stop and they did.

My daily routine was to first review the clipping service package to see if there were any articles addressing aviation. If there was, I was supposed to create a paragraph response that the President might use and submit it to the WH press office by 11:00 each day. They would then review all the paragraphs submitted from staffers like me and select what the press office would use at the press briefing that afternoon. A few of my words did end up coming from the President. The remainder of the day I would work on various work assignments and touch base with my contacts in the agencies to learn what they were seeing and doing.

Working in the WH had unexpected perks. Just working in the building was special. I remember one rainy afternoon, I heard some clicking in the hallway outside our office door. As I went out into the hallway to see what the noise was I saw a secret service agent walking Buddy the Presidents dog along the hallway. He told me that it was too wet to take the dog out for a long walk so our floor was the perfect place for some exercise. Another perk was observing the WH Easter-Egg Hunt. We were able to go out on the lawn to watch the festivities and each employee received a WH Egg with the President's signature and date. We were also invited to be part of the crowd for formal state visits on the lawn. We could watch the President greet the foreign dignitaries, wave flags, and see the bands march and play. We could also occasionally stand near the presidential helicopter to see the President return from his trips.

One of the best perks was having head-of-the-line privileges for WH tours. Before 9/11 people could simply show up at the White House between certain hours and stand in line to tour the ground and main floors of the house. Some days the lines nearly circled the WH grounds. There was a separate staff line near the entrance where any WH staffer could show his or her badge and go right into the tour line at the entrance. This made staffers like me very popular because you could also bring a friend. I got to the point where I could provide a very informative tour myself for family and friends. Unfortunately those days ended on 9/11.

The last perk that I will mention is the opportunity to sit in the Presidential Box at the Kennedy Center. As a non-political appointee my priority to receive such a perk was very low. However, they would make exceptions if you were having a special event. I applied for tickets for my wedding anniversary in the hopes that Kathie and I could go together and experience the Presidential Box. There was no response to my request, so I made dinner reservations for us to go out to dinner after work. At about 4:00, the Science Advisor's secretary called me up to her desk and gave me a red envelop that invited us into the Box that night at 7:00. I was excited. I called and told Kathie that our dinner out would need to be postponed and that she should dress for the Kennedy Center. She was excited too. I took the subway home and ran to greet Kathie to take her to the show. When I entered she asked me what we were going to see? I told her that I didn't know, but we were privileged to go. She told me that she had looked in the paper and could not find anything playing. At any rate, we took off to drive to the Kennedy Center.

When we arrived in the parking lot, there were lots of cars and hundreds of people in beautiful native Indian dress. This all seemed puzzling to us, but we proceeded to the ramp we were to go to and presented our invitation. As we approached the ramp to the Presidential Box, we saw a red velvet rope and an attendant. He immediately recognized the envelope and ushered us into the Box. The Box is actually a small room for people to gather, then there is a door that leads to the Box where you can see into the theatre. The box itself has about three rows of 4 chairs in the balcony. Inside the anti-room is a refrigerator with small bottles of champagne and boxes of M&Ms with a White House seal instead of an M on them. We were early so we helped ourselves to one of each and looked out into the audience. The entire theatre was filled with formally dressed people from India. Soon a military officer and his date and an FBI agent and his wife joined us. We took our seats and waited for the show to start.

To our surprise, a person who was obviously the master of ceremonies came out from behind the curtain and began speaking to the audience. Not a word of English. After that, the orchestra began to play discordant sounds and a woman emerged from behind the curtain to thunderous applause. She began singing along with the music. She sang song after song to the great enjoyment of the audience and our bewilderment. We later found out that she is the Ella Fitzgerald of India. About thirty minutes into the performance both of the other couples bailed out leaving us as the only people sitting in the Box. We felt as though we couldn't leave because we didn't want to offend the people in the audience who would look back at us and wonder who we were. What would it mean if the President's representatives didn't want to stay to hear this fabulous show? We did leave during intermission after about an hour and a half. This was our unforgettable experience sitting in the Presidents Box at the Kennedy Center. It was a memorable anniversary for sure.

GPS: One of my responsibilities was to be in charge of GPS for OSTP. The Global Positioning System (GPS) is a constellation of satellites that send out a time signal that can be received by ground station units. The baseline satellite constellation consists of 24 satellites positioned in six earth-centered orbital planes with four operational satellites and a spare satellite slot in each orbital plane. GPS ground receivers can receive signals from any of the satellites within view. Triangulating on the satellites and calculating the time variances can determine the position of the GPS unit. As the receiver unit moves in space its altitude, speed, and direction can be calculated and displayed. Of course you already know this because you undoubtedly have at least one.

The extremely accurate GPS that you use today to navigate your car, find places on your Smart Phone, and see the time almost anywhere was not very accurate prior to May 2000. The reason was for national security. The US Air Force put the GPS constellation in place for military purposes. There was an initial fear that our enemies would use it to target us so they installed a mechanism to dither the time signal to reduce its accuracy. This mechanism was called "selective availability" because the military could make it accurate or not depending on if selective availability was on or off.

Unfortunately for the military, the receivers that could provide accurate information when selective availability was on were very expensive so they provided the troops with commercial GPS units that were much cheaper. What the military discovered after the first Iraq war was that Saddam Hussein's first indication of an American invasion was that we turned off selective availability. The military also realized the tremendous day to day benefits of having an accurate GPS system and that they had the ability to jam the signal if need be in warfare. These realizations opened the door to considering GPS for civil use.

When I reported to OSTP, the Departments of Transportation and Commerce had formed a team to focus on civil GPS use. As the WH focal point, I was asked to oversee the coordination efforts and connect with the National Security Council that was the WH focal point for military GPS use. As things progressed there was a decision to try to eliminate selective availability and offer accurate GPS to the world. Betsy Pimentel from NSC and I were charged with preparing a decision package for the President. We jointly put the decision package together, created the talking points for the decision-makers, and crafted the press releases and release strategy. Her initial focus was to get the Joint Chiefs to sign off on the package and I handled the civil federal agencies. After much discussion and wordsmithing we had a final package ready for the President to sign.

During our interactions with the GPS community we discovered that there was an international GPS conference that was to be held on May 20 in Spain. That would be the perfect place to make the announcement. We were also told that the administration wanted the announcement to highlight civil use not military so we wanted a civil federal official to make the announcement in Spain. Dan Golden, the NASA Administrator, was chosen to make the announcement. Our announcement strategy was for Dan to fly to Spain in the FAA Gulfstream 4 aircraft the evening of May 19th from Washington National Airport so he could make the announcement on May 20th at the conference.

Everything was set on May 19, 2000. All the papers were developed, Dan Golden was in the airplane, the US Embassy in Spain was ready to rush him to the meeting and arrange for his participation, media releases were ready to go out, and official spokespersons ready to speak. The only thing missing was the signature of the President on the decision package.

The package was on President Clinton's desk and his secretary was ready to inform Betsy and I when he signed it, but it was now 5:00 PM on Friday afternoon. Betsy and I looked at each other. "What are the chances that the President would wander into his office late Friday afternoon to do paperwork"? We watched 6:00 go by. We could imagine what Dan Golden was thinking. At 6:45 we got the call. The President had returned to the office and signed our package!! We launched Dan, alerted the agencies, and sent notices for the press to release the next day. The rest is literally history.

Today accurate GPS is a key part of the world's infrastructure. It is facilitating technical advances and growing untold numbers of jobs from driverless cars, to drones, to smart anything. All this came from a military program that the President decided could be offered to the world free for civil use.

National Aviation Policy: In the final days of any administration the scientific and technical work in OSTP begins to wind down. There is just no time for new initiatives and existing activities come to a close. That was the perfect time for me to work on an initiative that I could present to the next administration. As a career civil servant, my position would not go away when the administration changed. I had been in a position to watch the Office of Management and Budget (OMB) and Congress make decisions about funding aviation R&D between DoD, NASA, and FAA. Each of these agencies get their funding from different congressional committees so it was easy for one committee to look at a particular program and say that another agency should do that justifying a cut in the budget of the agency for which they were responsible. I could also see that different agencies were tackling similar problems so it would be good to coordinate aviation efforts and policies between agencies.

The White House is able to decide what agency should focus on what, however, there was no "Presidential Decision Directive" (PDD) defining responsibilities. I decided to engage on this issue and drafted a PDD to form a group under the National Science and Technical Council (NSTC) to create such a policy.

I waited until the new administration came into office to present them with my proposal and a draft implementation document. My boss and the new Science Advisor liked the idea so they signed the document forming the NSTC group. Then all hell broke loose.

The new Deputy Secretary of the Department of Transportation's (DOT) became angry. In his view, aviation policy was the DOT's exclusive domain. I tried to explain to the Secretary that we were addressing issues above and between agencies not within agencies, but outrage won and the initiative was killed. The result was that OSTP withdrew the document and I was in hot water. I am happy to say that cooler heads prevailed after I left the White House. OSTP took up the idea and the President's Science Advisor (the same person who killed my effort) created and published the policy[ii].

George W. Bush 2001 Inauguration: About a week before the inauguration an Email went out to all members of the White House staff, that we were to move out of our offices by January 19, 2001 unless we were not political appointees and had official business to perform on inauguration day January 20th. I wasn't and I did so I decided to come into my office in the EEOB that day. I also invited Kathie to join me. It was an experience I will never forget.

On the morning of the inauguration, Saturday, January 20th, Kathie and I took the subway to the Farragut West stop and began to walk down 17th street. It was cold, raining, and windy. Hundreds of people were lining Pennsylvania Avenue to see the inaugural parade and to get a glimpse of the new President even though the motorcade was not to begin until after noon. We pushed through the crowd to the security guard and presented him with my credential. He let us pass. We then arrived at the 17th Street entrance of the OEOB and went through security again there to enter the building.

As we entered the building we noticed that there was not a soul around and all the office doors were open on the first floor where all the important offices are located. We went to my office on the 4th floor, checked my email, and decided to go for a tour. It was a fabulous opportunity. All the doors that are normally closed to all but the most important appointees were open to us. We could see the offices with the fireplaces, the only way to heat the building in the 1800s. We also saw the desks and computers in the offices piled into the hallways and corners of the rooms. We assumed that workmen must have done this. We realized that this weekend was the only time that maintenance could be done in the offices because on Monday morning everything needed to be set up for President Bush's Directors and staff. The carpets had been removed from some offices to be replaced and painters had prepared the rooms for painting.

We didn't realize it at the time, but we were witnesses to the "keyboard W scandal". As you might remember, the new administration discovered vandalism and that the Ws had been removed on their computer keyboards. There was an investigation to find out who did it. It wasn't us. I will say in hindsight, it did appear to be vandalism and that who ever left the computers piled on the floors disgraced this sacred building and the office of the President. Here is what the NY Times had to say:

WASHINGTON, June 11, 2002— The General Accounting Office, an investigative arm of Congress, said today that "damage, theft, vandalism and pranks did occur in the White House complex" in the presidential transition from Bill Clinton to George W. Bush. The agency put the cost at $13,000 to $14,000, including $4,850 to replace computer keyboards, many with damaged or missing W keys.

"A Secret Service report documented the theft of a presidential seal that was 12 inches in diameter from the Eisenhower Executive Office Building," next to the White House, on Jan. 19, 2001, the accounting office said.

We were not aware of all this at the time and simply thought the disarray was part of preparing for the new Presidential staff so we continued our tour.

After a trip back to my office we walked around the fourth floor where my office was located. About half way around the building we came to room 450. Room 450 is the Presidential auditorium. The largest room in the White House West Wing is the Roosevelt room. This room is set up for meetings and press events, but will only hold about 35 people. If the WH needs more room they use room 450 in the EEOB. It is a small auditorium with a stage that seats a couple of hundred people.

As we walked into the room we could see that the room was empty yet had a huge projection screen TV showing the inauguration ceremonies as they were being televised live from the Capitol. It was like having a front row seat. At the back of the room is a set of floor to ceiling curtained windows. As we pulled the curtains away we could see that the windows looked over Pennsylvania Avenue. How wonderful. We could sit in the room and watch the festivities on TV until the parade approached the White House, then look out the window to see the real thing live. As Kathie and I congratulated ourselves for being so fortunate, a man appeared from behind the curtains on the stage and asked who we were?

I thought the jig was up. I walked down to the stage to introduce myself hoping that I wasn't in any trouble. He introduced himself and told us that the room had been set up for the use of the heavy donors in case they wanted to get out of the rain, but that none had showed up. He seemed pleased that at least we were enjoying the fruits of his labors. After some discussion about what I did for OSTP and he did for WH Events, he told us that we should go down to the Indian Treaty Room where there was a luncheon buffet set up for all the people who didn't come.

The Indian Treaty Room was originally the library for the Department of the Navy. In the original building the Navy, Army, and State Department each had their own libraries. The Navy's library has been turned into an elegant reception room. As Kathie and I entered we saw three long tables of food and soft drinks with about six people in white waiter uniforms standing behind the tables. I felt a bit embarrassed for us and them, but walked up and told the waiter that the fellow in room 450 told us to come down to get something to eat. They served us and we took the delicious lunch back to room 450 to watch the show. By now the rain was pelting down, but we sat high and dry to see the entire inauguration first hand. Afterward, I returned to my office to finish up some work and we made our way home.

NextGen: Having failed at my attempt at creating a national aviation policy, I decided to take on America's Air Traffic Management System (ATMS). I was still convinced that bringing federal agencies together to address major problems was the solution. No single agency is empowered to work to develop a multi-agency effort. It needed to come from OSTP.

It was apparent that the next ATMS needed to be able to handle many more aircraft and that the GPS system that was now extremely accurate was the key. Switching from air traffic control (ATC) where surveillance of the aircraft's position came from the ATC radar to a system where the aircraft would broadcast its position was the key. The idea was that ATC could receive the aircraft GPS position and intent based on a flight plan stored in the aircraft computer. GPS position, speed, and time to each waypoint on the flight plan could be transmitted from the aircraft to ATC and other aircraft resulting in a much more efficient and safer aviation system. This new ATMS would provide much greater flexibility and greater use of automation both in the cockpit and on the ground. All of this, however, would require new equipment in every aircraft and for ATC on the ground.

As I looked at this problem it occurred to me that the DoD alone had about 16,000 aircraft whereas the U.S. commercial aircraft fleet was only about 7,000 not including general aviation. Military aircraft have to be able to fly in civil airspace. The DoD was already using an ATMS similar to what was needed in civil aviation so it made sense to me that we should get the DoD to simplify one of their existing systems for civil use that would be compatible with their system rather than design a new system and require DoD to equip its fleet with an additional system. Installing new civil system equipment would not only be very difficult to install in space-constrained fighter jets, but it would also be very expensive to acquire and integrate the new system into its existing warfare systems.

This led me to the idea of creating a "Joint Planning and Development Office" (JPDO) of all the federal civil and defense agencies. This office would develop an integrated plan for research and implementation of the next generation ATMS.

I had begun to meet with aviation association leaders to discuss this concept when I learned that I would be leading a Presidential Commission on the Future of the U.S. Aerospace Industry. This was the perfect opportunity to give this idea broad visibility.

The Full Monte: Once again I ran into problems for being innovative, this time with the FAA Acting Deputy Administrator, Monte Belger. As you may recall, I had been on detail from the FAA during all my work at NASA and the WH. On Good Friday 2002, I got a call from the FAA telling me that I was being recalled to the FAA. No reason was given. After setting up the Aerospace Commission, they wanted to pull me back to FAA without any clear assignment. I replied that I was under orders from the President's Science Advisor to manage the Commission. Their response was to begin insubordination action against me. I told the Commission Chair, former Congressman Bob Walker. He was outraged. "How dare they do this to my Executive Director". Congressman Walker called the Secretary of Transportation, Norm Mineta. The FAA rescinded their recall. I owe Bob Walker and Secretary Mineta my reputation and probably my federal retirement.

As it turned out, the Commissioners embraced the idea of a JPDO and made the idea of a multi-agency developed ATMS a recommendation in their final report. In the end, the Congress acted on the Commission report and created the JPDO and the ATMS concept that became known as NextGen. The DoT and FAA have now fully embraced NextGen and are pursuing its implementation.

There are three lessons to be learned from this:
1. Government officials get angry if you challenge their discretion even if the challenge is a good idea.
2. If there is an issue worth challenging a government official about, be prepared to be fired, fined, jailed, or worse. (Ron Heifetz is right.)
3. If what you are fighting for is worthwhile, it will be achieved in the end, if not by you then someone else.

Aerospace Commission: At the end of the Clinton administration, Congress passed an act establishing the Presidential Commission on the Future of the U.S. Aerospace Industry that was to begun in 2001, the first year of the Bush administration. After the new OSTP leadership settled in, they appointed me to be the Executive Director of the Commission. I was responsible for establishing and managing the Commission day to day under the leadership of the Chair, Bob Walker, who was appointed by the President. It was a huge task. The Congress had provided no funding yet we needed to find office space, computers, staff, public hearing rooms, etc, and follow all the federal regulations concerning federal advisory groups. It was like creating a small government agency in a few months.

The best part of working on the Commission was the people involved. The President and both houses of Congress and political parties selected the commissioners. They were a remarkable group of distinguished individuals who have a passion for improving America's aerospace industry.

Presidential appointees
- Buzz Aldrin - Former Astronaut & second man to walk on the Moon
- Ed Bolen – President, General Aviation Manufacturers Association at that time
- John W. Douglass - Former Assistant Secretary of the Navy & CEO of AIA
- Neil deGrasse Tyson – Astrophysicist & Director of the Hayden Planetarium
- Robert S. Walker - Former U.S. Representative from Pennsylvania and House Science Committee Chair
- Heidi Wood - Managing Director, Morgan Stanley

Senate appointees
- John Hamre – CEO, Center for Strategic and International Studies (CSIS)
- William Schneider, Jr. – Consultant to Donald Rumsfeld Secretary of Defense
- Robert J. Stevens - Chairman, President, and CEO of Lockheed Martin

House appointees
- Tom Buffenbarger – President, International Association of Machinists
- F. Whitten Peters-- Former Secretary of the Air Force
- Tillie K. Fowler – Former U.S. Representative from Florida

I was extremely fortunate to connect with Paul Piscopo at the DOD who was able to pull the logistics and most of the staff together. He also helped me to eventually secure funding from DOD. Paul became my office manager and indispensable member of the Commission. My other key person was Dr. Fenton Carey who was my right hand policy advisor and writer who pulled all the different parts of the commission writings together into a coherent and well-organized final document.

There were many notable events that occurred during the Commission, but one is most noteworthy and it occurred before our first public hearing on November 27, 2001; the 9/11 aviation attack on America.

9/11: On the morning of September 11, 2001 I was holding a Commission staff meeting at our offices on the top floor of Crystal Gateway 1 in Crystal City. There were representatives from all the federal agencies having anything to do with aviation or space along with my permanent staff.

As I spoke to the group about the issues of the day my pager went off. Yes, I said my pager. It is hard to believe today, but cell phones were not commonplace and OSTP had issued me a pager. I excused myself from the meeting and called my office. The secretary told me that Richard needed me to call him immediately and gave me his number. Richard was my immediate boss so I did. I never got through to him. About this time someone from a neighboring office came bursting into our conference room and announced that a plane had just hit the World Trade Center in NYC. Then I knew why Richard was calling; because I was the Aviation Advisor in the White House.

I assumed at that point that it must be an airline accident. As I continued to try to contact Richard and debating what to do, we heard a loud thud and saw the smoke from the Pentagon out the window. Someone from an adjacent office came in to tell us that a plane had hit the Pentagon. I had flown the approach to Reagan Airport many times and couldn't believe that a plane would be flying so low. Then it became clear... America was under attack.

I told everyone that I was headed to the WH on the subway. As I reached the platform, however, the subway was closed down. The subway runs through the Pentagon just one stop from Crystal City where our office was located. I returned to our meeting room and went in search of an office that had a TV (no smart-phones yet). Finally we saw the reports of the World Trade Center towers and the Pentagon and heard that there was another airplane perhaps aimed at the White House, so it and the Capitol were being evacuated. I told everyone to go home.

My only option to get home at that point was to walk or the subway, so I went back to the Metro. By that time the Metro was running trains back and forth from Crystal City to the end of the line opposite the Pentagon on both sets of tracks. I ended up getting a train on the normally wrong side of the track and got back to Alexandria where I could walk home. Kathie and I spent the afternoon glued to the TV along with most of the rest of America and the world.

The next day, I took the Metro to the Farragut West Station as usual to go to my office at the White House. As I emerged from the subway I could see barriers set up across 17th street and a security gate. All the roads around the White House complex were closed down. When I entered the building I could feel an electric energy within the staff. At my office, I began to collect information from all the agencies I worked with. I even catalogued all the responses from the Gore Commission that addressed aviation security in case it would be helpful. By then, all the civil aircraft in the country had been grounded by Secretary Mineta, so I began to field inquiries from the aviation industry about what would happen next and when could their flights get back up and running.

President Bush turned to National Security Advisor Condoleezza Rice to lead the national response effort. She called on one of her staff, Richard Clark. This was Richard Clark's time in the sun. I immediately sent him an internal email identifying myself as the aviation advisor in OSTP, provided him with a summation of the information available, and offered to help him in any way he liked. I got no response. I called his office to ensure that I had the correct email address and asked if I could talk to him. The address was correct and he was not available to talk. I went down to his office on the third floor just a floor below and a few doors down the corridor from mine, but they would not let me in. Clark, a counter terrorism expert, made all the White House decisions affecting aviation without any technical aviation insights as far as I could tell.

A minor example of the adverse affects of this narrow focus was the blimp industry. An edict was issued that no aircraft would be allowed to fly over large groups of people. That edict almost bankrupted the blimp industry whose livelihood depends on flying advertising and TV cameras over sporting events. Their representatives came in to see me to see if I could help. They pointed out that a blimp is a perfect surveillance platform and that they would be delighted if the FBI or police wanted to use them for security monitoring at large events. I was eventually able to get them some relief, but it wasn't easy.

As it turned out a female Air Force Lt. Colonel who coordinated aircraft activities at the FAA ATC Command Center was the first to recognize that America was under attack. She immediately called General Eberhart, the Commander of the North American Defense Command. I was told from a personal friend and knowledgeable source, that General Eberhart called the FAA Deputy Administrator his point of contact and then the office of the Secretary of Transportation and told them that they needed to bring down the civil aviation fleet so that the military could identify any rogue aircraft or, "The Air Force would shoot them down". While I don't think that would ever happen, the Secretary did shut down civil aviation the day of the attack and for many days thereafter.

Working with the Aerospace Commissioners: One of the greatest joys of my federal career was working with the commissioners of the Aerospace Commission. They all gave freely of their time without pay to lay out the baseline of aerospace in America and make recommendations to support a better future. The first public meeting of the Commission was November 27 2001 and the final report was issued to the President on November 18, 2002. During the Commission, we went to Cape Canaveral to see a Shuttle launch, to Colorado to see the Space Foundation exposition, to Europe to meet with the European Union and attend the Farnborough Air-show in England, to Russia to tour Star City, (Russia's space center), and meet with Russian officials, and to China to meet with two government leaders for major manufacturing (AVIC 1 & 2). Along the way and during our DC meetings, I had the pleasure to really get to know each of the commissioners. A lot of things that were said and done during the Commission were confidential, but a couple of vignettes might give you a glimpse of what it was like.

Bob Walker: I became very close to our Chairman, Bob Walker. He runs a high-power consulting firm since retiring from the Congress. It was a real experience walking the halls of Congress with him. Everyone that passed said hello and called him by name. Bob is a visionary and an innovator. He would tell me about his belief that hydrogen fuel cells would one day replace gasoline in cars. When hydrogen burns it produces water. Hydrogen fuel cells produce electricity to power electric vehicles. So, hydrogen fuel cell cars are not only environmentally friendly but you can fill them up like gasoline based cars so no charging stations are necessary. He also said that of all the heavenly bodies near Earth that we should explore, Europa, a moon of Jupiter, probably has liquid water under its surface so it has the greatest chance for supporting life beyond Earth. Many scientists are supporting these conclusions today. Bob is also an extremely skilled leader.

As we neared the end of the Commission we asked each commissioner to provide us with six recommendations that they thought the Commission should adopt. We asked for their response prior to attending a one day meeting to create the final recommendations for the report. My thought was that this would result in similar recommendations from the commissioners so it would not be hard to get agreement. The reality was the Commissioners submitted a total of 125 different recommendations. Each had a powerful advocate. I was in panic mode. We had agreed to have no more than 10 recommendations. How could I get the group from 125 to 10 in one meeting? Bob had the answer.

The next morning Bob had a draft set of recommendations from his review of what was submitted and handled the meeting like a congressional markup. Each commissioner could comment on each of Bob's recommendations and the group adjusted them according to the discussion. This resulted in changes to his document, but agreement on ten recommendations, as we wanted.

Buzz Aldrin: Buzz is an amazing guy. It was truly incredible for me to travel around the world with Buzz, the international celebrity. Everywhere we went people wanted to meet him, take a picture with him, and hear what he had to say. He is gracious to all. What he has had to say since his walk on the moon is to challenge America to have a robust space exploration program. It is a travesty that the US has to pay the Russians to send our astronauts to the International Space Station. Buzz has dedicated his life to encouraging us to build the next great space ship, expand the space frontier, and go to Mars. He is not only a spokesman, but he has developed a series of specific proposals pointing the way to a future in space that will benefit the earth as well. Anyone who has gone to space becomes an advocate for America's space program, but no one has put more energy and dedication into space exploration than Buzz Aldrin.

Neil deGrasse Tyson: Neil is an astrophysicist and educator. He is a joy to know. He is undoubtedly the single most inspiring scientist in America today. Many people know him from his PBS and other TV appearances, however he is on advisory boards for NASA and DoD where he is making real contributions to their efforts today. I am honored to call him friend. Seeing the aerospace activities around the US and the world through his eyes was enlightening and entertaining. His insights and sense of humor kept the commission thinking and lightened times of stress. One example of this was during a two day offsite meeting to narrow what we would address as a commission.

Think about having 11 experienced and creative commissioners locked in a conference room, trying to come together on what should be done and said in a report covering the entire aerospace industry consisting of air, space, civil, military, government management, contracting, industrial policy, workforce education, and research and development. After the first day of the meeting we needed to get out into the fresh air and unwind. As we were walking the beautiful grounds of the retreat facility at night, with a full display of stars above, Neil started an impromptu lecture of what we were seeing in the heavens above. That somehow put our meeting discussions into perspective and brought us closer together. After his lecture he showed us something that we could all learn that I will share with you.

He pointed to the cars in the parking lot and asked us to press our door lock remote to see if we could unlock our car from where we were standing. Well, we were too far away and we heard no bleeping. Then he told us to hold the remote by our throat, open our mouth to make a make an OH with our lips, and press the button again while facing the car. The locks opened. He showed us how we could focus the energy in our car door beepers through our mouths just as astronomers focus their radio telescopes. It works.

Bill Schneider: The last vignette I will mention is a discussion I had with Bill Schneider at Henry VIII's Hampton Court, England. We spent all day at the Farnborough Air Show talking to aerospace companies and dignitaries from around the world. It was evening and we had finished dinner at the reception at Hampton Court. I walked out into the gardens on a picture perfect night. The garden was discretely lit under the trees along the pathways. As I walked reflecting on all that we had seen and heard, I saw Bill sitting on one of the benches. I sat down beside him and told him that my plan after the Commission was to retire from the government and set up a consulting firm. I asked him to reflect on his consulting career and give me his advice. He said, "Don't use your home address". I didn't.

We of course all knew the threat of developing a Commission Report that would sit on a shelf without impact. I am delighted to say that our commission had results. The President picked up on our recommendation to go back to the Moon and Mars as a goal for the space program. Congress enacted our NextGen ideas. Our focus on STEM education to prepare a workforce for the future gained acceptance and is now a major education theme. Other recommendations became substantiation for federal agency budget requests and were integrated into programs. Beyond this, our report was the first and only comprehensive documentation and baseline for America's most important industry. It was a tremendous honor to be involved.

My Government Career Ends: After the release of the final Commission report Paul Piscopo and I spent the next month disassembling the commission office space and closing out our contracts. I retired from the government on January 3, 2003 after almost 34 years of government service. Looking back, I see myself as an innovator and government entrepreneur who, along with a lot of hard-working associates, moved aviation toward a better future. I was blessed to be able to see what needed to be done and be in a position to initiate change. If the change needed to be made in a different agency, I went there. The Commission allowed the Commissioners and me to lay out a path to the future for aerospace for our country and we are on that path today.

Epilogue

So if you think that my life has been somewhat amazing and filled with coincidences that turned out well, let me tell you why. I firmly believe that God has been working in my life from the beginning to make it so.

To begin with, as a very premature baby in 1946 I probably shouldn't have lived. But it is what happened to me during my life that has taken me on a spiritual journey along with the physical and career journey just described. In this epilogue, I will describe a few of the countless interactions that I have had with God's Holy Spirit along the way that led me to the life I have had and to a close personal relationship with God. My life is a testimony to what you can experience if you love God and others, work hard, and have faith that He will turn your efforts into positive results in ways you would never imagine.

Age 15: I was 15 years old and a member of my high school wrestling team. It was February, about 5:30 p.m., cold and dark. I was walking home about a half mile from the school on a lonely sidewalk. I could see my breath and having showered after practice my hair and ears were freezing. As I started to climb the hill before me, the cold and the fatigue from the practice started to get to me. Without even thinking I said a little prayer under my breath. "Dear Lord, it sure is cold." Then the Holy Spirit touched me. A wave of warmth spread across me from my toes to my head. I knew that God had answered my prayer. I started to run. I couldn't contain myself. I thanked God and ran the rest of the way home. I burst into the kitchen where my mother was cooking dinner and announced, " I am going to be a minister." That event is as clear to me today as it was then. And, while I did not become a minister, from that day on I have been sure that God hears our prayers. He is concerned and involved in events here on earth. He lives and loves us.

Ben & the Car Radio: Not too long after my initial experience with the Holy Spirit, my friend Ben came to me to tell me that his mother's car radio wasn't working right. I had distinguished myself in the neighborhood as a person who could make minor electrical repairs. I had a budding TV business where I would take the tubes (yes tubes) out of neighbor's TVs, label where I took them from, and take them to the hardware store to the tube tester. There I could find the bad tubes, buy new ones, and replace them for twice the price of the tubes pocketing the profit. I also got good at using tuner cleaner, a spray that cleans the contacts of analogue tuners in the sets so that the channels would come in clear. After such notoriety, Ben came to me with a request. The pushbutton radio in his mother's car wasn't working properly and would not lock onto the appropriate frequency. He asked me if I would fix it. Sounded like a case for tuner cleaner to me so I agreed to try.

After a great deal of effort we removed the huge radio from the car and brought it to my father's basement workshop. As we took the back off of the set I saw that it was nothing like anything I had ever seen before. The pushbuttons were attached to carbon rods the diameter of a pencil and by a brass rod and screw that adjusted how far the rod would move when the button was pushed. When a button was pushed the rod would slide a specific distance into a tube that would result in the right frequency being selected. I had no idea what to do. I told Ben that we needed to just close it back up and put it back in the car before his mother found out. With that, he reached in and broke one of the carbon rods. I was mortified. How would I ever explain this to his mother and to mine?

I began to pray most earnestly. All I can say is that I knew that God would hear my prayer because He had before. Then it dawned on me that I had an old car radio I had picked up in a junkyard. Perhaps there was a part in it that would help. There was. It was not the same model radio, but I was able to adapt the carbon rod and put it into Ben's mother's radio. My heart was pounding when it seemed to fit, but would it work? YES!

You might just chalk this up to luck or ingenuity, but I knew that God had helped me, strengthening my belief.

"Behind the Bleachers" Dream: I am sure some reading this have had dreams of having fun behind the bleachers of a basketball court. My dream was not about fun. It is still clear in my mind after all these years since High School. In the dream, I go down behind the bleachers during a basketball game and am confronted by another kid with a knife comes at me to kill me. I can still sense the panic. Then in the dream, I realize that the God of the Universe is with me. At that thought, the attacker vanishes and a great sense of peace came over me. I believe that this dream was sent by God to tell me that I have nothing to fear because He is with me.

This insight gave me the strength to become a pilot, fly in the Vietnam War, move forward into the unknown, and stand up for what I believe is right in my career. Perhaps you can see through these three stories how God has gradually made Himself known to me and guided my spiritual development. But he didn't stop there.

In the Pool in the Bahamas – My Baptism: In the summer of 1967 the TKE fraternity held its annual conclave at the Grand Bahama Hotel, in the Bahamas. I was not part of my chapter's official delegation but went along to be with my friends. The conclave was in August prior to my 21st birthday that October. One funny story, of the trip was when we went from the hotel to Freeport where they had gambling casinos. My friends were older than me so they wanted to try their luck. So did I. As we walked onto the casino floor two security guards started to follow me. I walked past the gaming tables to the slot machine area. They followed me. I knew that they were following me, but I just had to pull one slot machine handle. As I put my nickel (yes a nickel) in the slot and pulled the handle the guards approached me and told me that I needed to leave. I asked why? They said that I needed to be 21 to gamble. My youthful look was once again getting me into trouble. I had to think fast... Well, I said, this is a gambling casino isn't it? They said yes. "Well I want to make you a bet." They looked puzzled. "I'll bet you that I will be 21 within 60 days. If I can prove that, you will let me stay. If I can't, I will leave peaceably. If you don't take the bet, I will leave kicking and screaming." I won the bet and stayed long enough to lose $5.

After my experience in Freeport, I returned to the hotel for the next two days. One late afternoon as the sun was going down I was in the hotel pool. As I floated on my back looking up at the sky I thought of all the blessings that God had given me. As I floated there I told God that I would dedicate my life to Him and asked him to lead me as he wanted. I believe he has. As I was writing this sentence it became clear to me that this was not just a statement of faith to God, but my baptism. I had been baptized as an infant, however, in looking back on the experience it has dawned on me now that I was on my back submerged in the water, being blessed / baptized by God.

Career Decision- I want to be an Airline Pilot: By the mid 1970's, I was off active duty and in the Air Force Reserves. I was an Air Force pilot with over 3,000 hours of heavy jet flying time, and my dream was to become an airline pilot. Unfortunately, none of the airlines were hiring, so I joined the FAA as an Air Carrier Operations Inspector. One day, I saw a notice that United Airlines would begin to hire its first pilot training class in 7 years. This was my chance. I called United's Chief Pilot at Washington National Airport and asked if I could meet with him. He agreed. This began one of my close encounters with the Holy Spirit.

On the day of my meeting, Kathie picked me up at FAA headquarters and drove me to United's office in a hangar at National Airport. There was an empty parking slot near the front door, so we parked and I went in to talk to the Chief Pilot. I described my aviation career with the military and FAA. I also told him that I had received B-747 training at United's training center in Denver and had an Airline Transport Pilot rating as a result. This was music to his ears. I had experience in large jets, with the FAA, the agency that regulates United, and I had proven myself to United's own training department in their most complicated aircraft. He gave me an application, put his initials at the top, and invited me to send it back to him personally. I was on cloud nine. If I could get into United's first training class in years, at my age, I could one day become their Chief Pilot. This was because all the pilots senior to me would one day be retired before me.

My head was spinning as I left the building and got back into my car. I joyfully told my wife what had happened and went to start the car. The battery was dead. When I turned the key, I could not even hear a click. I couldn't believe it. We had just driven and parked 15 minutes before. As I was trying to figure out what to do, someone stopped and asked me if they could help me jump-start the car. I gratefully agreed. After the car started, my wife drove me back to work and returned home. We never had battery trouble in that car again. This, however, was only the first of a series of unusual events that followed the interview.

That evening I completed the United Airlines pilot application with great enthusiasm. At that point, I began to feel uncomfortable. I decided that I would wait until the next day and review the application again. Perhaps my uncomfortable feeling was because I had done something wrong on the application and I would discover what it was when I reviewed it with fresh eyes. The uneasiness continued the next day at work, so I was anxious to get back to the application when I got home. That evening, I reviewed the application again, but could not find any problems. So, I put it in the envelope, added several stamps so it surely had enough postage, and went out the front door to mail the application at the mailbox on the corner... I could not put the application into the mailbox.

As I opened the mailbox, my uneasiness turned to dread. That is the only way I can describe it. Like the feeling you have when you hear that a loved one has died. I backed away from the mailbox and brought the application back home. If I had known the things I am writing about in this paper, I would have known that this was from the Holy Spirit, but I didn't understand at the time. I thought that I should simply give it some time.

I went to work the next day and received a call from my boss at the FAA. He told me that I had been selected to enter an executive training program that would lead to my becoming a member of the federal Senior Executive Service and a position of responsibility. This came out of the blue at the precise time I was wrestling with the decision to apply to United.

That night was a restless one for me. My dream had been to become an airline pilot. How could I simply walk away from this fabulous opportunity? Work only 15 days a month, much higher salary than FAA, free airline passes- "I am a sucker to turn this down". Yet something wasn't right. That brought me to the Bible and prayer. I don't remember what I read or said to God. There was no burning bush or vision, just a gentle calm as I decided to accept the FAA's offer. I sometimes think you don't know what the right decision is until after you make it. But, in this case I am sure that the Holy Spirit was guiding me.

As it turned out, many of my friends did become airline pilots. Under the FAA regulations, they were forced to retire when they became age 60. Their timing was such that they reached 60 in 2006. If you recall, the airlines were all in deep financial trouble at that time and had unfunded retirement programs. One of my airline pilot friends had earned a $95,000 a-year retirement that was slashed to $23,000.

I, on the other hand, had many unbelievable opportunities to improve aviation safety, contribute to our country's aerospace industry, be the Aviation Policy Advisor in the White House on 9/11, and retire from government with a great government pension. I certainly wouldn't have guessed that this would be the outcome in 1977.

AeroClub Luncheon: I would like to expand on the story I told earlier about my going to NASA. I was unexpectedly asked to sit at the head table at an AeroClub luncheon between the Administrator who had gutted the authority of my office by saying that he would not side with the Safety Office over a Program office and the Administrator who decided not to select me to run the Safety Office. As the luncheon program began, the President of the Club, most amazingly, introduced me first. He asked me to stand up behind the head table, told those at the luncheon of my many successes for aviation safety, called me Mr. FAA Safety, and asked for a round of applause. While this was extremely flattering, what came to me was that I was living the 23rd Psalm.

Psalms 23:4-6 (KJV)
4 Yea, though I walk through the valley of the shadow of death, I will fear no evil: for thou art with me; thy rod and thy staff they comfort me.
5 Thou preparest a table before me in the presence of mine enemies: thou anointest my head with oil; my cup runneth over.
6 Surely goodness and mercy shall follow me all the days of my life: and I will dwell in the house of the LORD forever.

While these Administrators were not my enemies, and my life was certainly not in danger, the parallel to the 23rd Psalm struck me as I stood behind the table being praised before the administrators and the audience. I felt that the Holy Spirit was giving me the experience of this Bible parable first hand within the context of my life. It helped to build my faith and encouraged me to persevere even during this time of adversity. This is an example of the work of the Bible and the Spirit coming together in my daily life.

Passed Over for Promotion: Just prior to the luncheon that I just described, FAA Administrator called me into his office and told me that he wanted to put another person from outside of the agency in as the head of the Safety Office that I had been successfully running for most of the past six years. By this time, I was keenly aware of the Holy Spirit working in my life and I couldn't understand why this was happening to me. Surely God would not have guided me into working for FAA only to leave me stuck in a position where I couldn't be effective until the end of my federal government career. He didn't. I made some of my greatest contributions as a result of leaving the FAA.

I bring up this story again because I truly believe that the Holy Spirit guided my life and my career. At a low point, when I felt all was over, an entirely new set of opportunities emerged that led me to experiences and contributions that I could not have dreamed of. At each step along the way, I felt the pull as I did when I was first guided into the FAA. Having my 23rd Psalm experience led to my transition to NASA, and then a series of airplane accidents brought me to the White House. I was the Aviation Advisor in the White House on September 11, 2001 when the planes hit the World Trade Center, Pentagon and field in Pennsylvania. I was honored to serve the nation in the White House at that important time.

Bottom Line: As events in my life and career occurred, I began to search for the context of what was happening to see if I could discern the input from the Holy Spirit. Perseverance and faith has kept me moving forward into the unknown. The hand of God through His Spirit has led me to the point where I am writing this book.

Revelation about Revelation: While I ended my autobiography when I left the government, the story of how God has worked in my live continues. After I retired from the government and set up my consulting firm, I had time to work on projects that interested me and more time digging into the Bible in order to try to explain all the acts of the Holy Spirit that I had experienced. I could see how active God was in my life and sought to understand it. This resulted in a burst of Spiritual insight that is captured in my book "Jesus Reveals Revelation". I will relate some of the process of this Spiritual insight to you as an example of how the Holy Spirit moved me.

"The Book of Revelation" is the last book in the Bible. If you haven't read it, take a look. As I pondered Revelation over the years it seemed incomprehensible. It appears to be written chronologically from the time of John forward to the next world. Yet the stories of the harlot, various beasts, plagues, etc. seemed to not tell a smooth flowing, understandable story. Many verses start with "Then" or contain "and then" which seemed to indicate that the next actions in the story followed the preceding. But, the text did not seem clear. On the other hand, Revelation is obviously a prophecy written to tell Christians throughout the centuries what will happen in advance so we will persevere and keep the faith. This contradiction between a book to tell Christians what will happen, yet presenting a book that is not clear, seemed to be a contradiction.

The admonition in Revelation 22:19 to "not take away any of the **words** of this prophecy", got me wondering why the focus on words? It begged the question, "If I had to consider and use every word of the prophecy to understand it, what could be changed that would provide me greater insight?" As I wrestled with how to understand these things, I connected Jesus' words in the Gospels when the apostles asked Him about the end of the age with the words in the Revelation text. As I assembled the relevant verses on the end times from across the Bible, the answer became clear. The words in Revelation are true, but the order of the events described is not. This is a way that God could give all mankind the same words to read over the ages yet seal up Revelation's full understanding until the end time. This is the hypothesis of my book "Jesus Reveals Revelation".

But why would John write Revelation out of order? The answer to this question is that he didn't. He wrote it in the order of the visions that God showed him. Rev 1:10 – 11, "I was in the Spirit on the Lord's day, and I heard behind me a loud voice like {the sound} of a trumpet, saying, 'Write in a book what you see, and send {it} to the seven churches". But I believe that God did not show John the events described in the order in which they would take place, thereby sealing up the Revelation prophecy until the end times. My spine tingled as I made this connection.

I believe that the Book of Revelation is the chronological prophecy of what John saw unfold as scenes in heaven, scenes on earth, flashbacks, and prophecies. The word "then" means what John saw next not necessarily what would happen next. John's experience is like watching a play where you see all the acts and scenes of the play, but not in order, and then you are told to write what you saw. It is only by reordering these scenes that the true chronology and prophecy emerges. But how should you reorder it? By basing it on what Jesus said to his disciples in the Gospels. Jesus, therefore, reveals the Revelation prophecy.

I believe that God did not want the true chronology to be known until the end times so that each generation would believe and look to the day of Christ's return, even if it was actually to be hundreds of years away. As we enter the end times, He wants us to know the straight story so that believers will be comforted, encouraged, and persevere.

As I wrote <u>Jesus Reveals Revelation</u> the scriptures began to open up and I received greater understanding as I wrote each subsequent draft. What emerged is an understandable end time prophecy and chronology with distinct subdivisions based on Jesus' words in the Gospels and God's involvement with his chosen people and recipients of His covenants, the Jews and the Christians. The prophecy also answers many questions that have puzzled mankind, such as what happens to us when we die and why a loving God would permit evil in the world.

Doctor's Office to Seminary: About three months after I published my book on Revelation I was sitting in my Doctor's office for my annual physical. The doctor came into the room and said, "I hear you have written a book about Revelation". I was amazed and asked how he knew thinking this was another action from God. It wasn't, but lead to one.

He told me that he had just examined my wife and she had told him about my book because she knew that he had done medical work for his church overseas. So his knowledge of my book was no insight, but what he had to say was. He told me that the Virginia Theological Seminary (VTS) located about 5 miles from my house, was starting a course on Revelation for evening students in about two weeks. He encouraged me to sign up and I did. That was a great blessing because it brought me to a place where I could gain an academic background to complement my personal studies, and gain additional insights that lead me to write my second book <u>The Word and the Spirit: How God Speaks to YOU</u>. I now have a Diploma in Theological Studies from VTS.

First National Aerospace Foreign Direct Investment Expo: This last story of how God has worked in my life occurred in my present occupation. As I write this, I am the Executive Director of the Aerospace States Association (ASA). ASA is an association of State Lt. Governors. ASA's goals are to promote the aerospace industry, foster economic development, grow aerospace jobs, and promote STEM education to create an aerospace workforce for the future. At the end of 2014, the U.S. Department of Commerce came to ASA to ask us to co-host an exposition to which they would bring aerospace related investors from overseas, and we would bring state economic development organizations to facilitate economic development in the States. The story of the Expo is a long one, but God's involvement is easy to tell.

The Expo was to be held in October 2015. ASA and our event planner had signed the agreements with the hotel and made all the logistical arrangements. California won the bid in the state competition to be the host state. All was going smoothly except the turnout. With three weeks to go before the opening date, we had hundreds of un-booked rooms that we were responsible to fill under our contract with the hotel. California let us down, the U.S. aerospace industry didn't show, and DoC brought less than a third of the investors that they had promised.

At that point I received a letter from the hotel that they had checked our credit rating and we had none. I of course knew this because we would never want to be in a position where the LT. Governors would owe money. The hotel letter went on to say that we would need to pay for the entire Expo up front or they would withdraw the facilities. Attached to the letter was an invoice for $234,169.47. We didn't have the funds. This was the culmination of months of hard work, hand wringing, and prayer. It looked like all was lost. How would I tell all the states that their investment was lost and the Lt. Governors that their association was going into bankruptcy? I had faith that God would help me, but I couldn't see how.

Our wonderful event manager went back to the hotel and argued that they could charge us for the Expo, but that it was unfair to charge us for the unused rooms up front as well. Fortunately the Hotel agreed and sent us a bill for the unpaid balance for the Expo of $103,427.67 with a note that we would be responsible for the unpaid rooms within 30 days of the event. We had $104,619 in the bank when we received the bill. My prayers were answered. We could pay for the Expo up front with only a little over $1,000 to spare in the bank. Many more people registered in the last two weeks before the event and we ended up paying the hotel only $41,413.80 for unused rooms. Those that attended the Expo cited it as a great success and we ended up with a small profit to pay our volunteers. I have no doubt that God helped me through this crisis. He will help you too. If you don't think so I suggest you read the following.

Disbelief: I am sure that you can see by now that I firmly believe that I have a personal relationship with God that He has fostered and promoted. As I learned to trust Him, I came to see that He is leading me. This section the book is written to people who do not believe in a Christian God and those who are unsure.

You see an earth that is full of evil, disasters, and things that a loving god would not allow if there were a god. You have seen horrible things done in the name of religion and hatred between different religious groups and religious people. Perhaps you have read the critics of the Bible and have been convinced that conflicting Biblical texts and uncertain authorship and interpretation render the Bible useless. Or perhaps you have turned to science where there are efforts to show that life and all that we know can exist without God. Because of this, you may view believers as disillusioned. On the other hand, you may sense that there is a spirit within you and others.

Your disbelief is probably based on your worldview framed by the Religion and family you grew up in, your education, friends, and your observations of a lifetime. What if there is a way to discover your connection to God that has not yet been proclaimed by churches? In the following, I propose to open your eyes to the purpose of your life and a remarkable set of insights that I want to share with you that, taken together, present a new paradigm for belief.

Background: Before we begin, I would like to make three points. First, that there is a distinction between God and religion. God is the almighty creator of the universe. Religion is mankind's attempt to understand God, interpret His will, and help people follow God's will and grow in God's love. Whoever interprets God's will on earth assumes God's power over those who believe the interpretation. There are some so-called churches and religious beliefs that only exist for that power and the fortune it brings.

The second point is that there is only one founder of a religion that claims to be God; not Abraham, not Moses, not Mohammad, not Buddha, etc. only Jesus Christ. If God is going to have a personal relationship with people, as he has with me, he must start somewhere. I believe He started with Abraham and Moses then revealed Himself as Jesus Christ. Other religions might be inspired and lead you to God as I will discuss later, but God revealed himself through Jesus Christ.

The third point is that there are probably only two authors in the New Testament (NT) of the Bible who are eyewitnesses to Jesus Christ and His revelations, John and Paul. John says at the beginning of his Gospel, Jesus' life is the living word of God. **Jesus is** the revelation that God sent us. It is His example as described in the Bible that we need to follow. I will later show how this relates to other religions.

God's Gospel is not a statement in text. It is the **act** of Jesus' life, crucifixion,[iii] and rising from the dead as Christ. That is the essence of Paul's Gospel from the revelation he received, but there is more that he reveals.

A New Paradigm For Belief: I propose three big picture concepts derived from Paul's revelations captured in the book of Romans that might help to explain God's plan and might help to inspire you to turn to Christ. These concepts include; the nature of the human spirit vs. the Holy Spirit, God's purpose for creating us, and understanding the physical and spiritual laws God chooses to operate under. Together, they form a new paradigm for understanding God's message to us.

1. Human Spirit vs. the Holy Spirit: I offer the thought that there is a distinction between the breath of life (physical life and spirit) that God gave all life as part of creation when He set the universe on its evolutionary course, and the eternal life-giving Spirit that comes from the indwelling of the Holy Spirit when a person accepts God's call. Each living part of creation has the spirit of its "kind" as described in Genesis Chapter 1. That spirit is different from God's Spirit that is given to people who are searching for God.

Let's see what Paul says about the spirit in Romans. I believe that his reference to the flesh is actually referring to the human spirit. Italics are my interpretations.

Romans 8:5-11 (NASB)[iv]

⁵ For those who are according to the flesh *(human spirit)* set their minds on the things of the flesh, but those who are according to the *(Holy)* Spirit, the things of the Spirit.
⁶ For the mind set on the flesh is death, but the mind set on the Spirit is life and peace,
⁷ because the mind set on the flesh is hostile toward God; for it does not subject itself to the law of God, for it is not even able *to do so,*

⁸ and those who are in the flesh *(working under the human spirit)* cannot please God.

⁹ **However, you are not in the flesh *(human spirit)* but in the *(Holy)* Spirit, if indeed the Spirit of God dwells in you. But if anyone does not have the Spirit of Christ, he does not belong to Him.**

¹⁰ If Christ is in you, though the body is dead because of sin, yet the (*human*) spirit is alive because of righteousness *(given through Christ's Spirit that joins with the human spirit in you)*.

¹¹ But if the Spirit of Him who raised Jesus from the dead dwells in you, He who raised Christ Jesus from the dead will also give life to your mortal bodies *(and human spirit)* through His Spirit who dwells in you.

Romans 8:16 (NASB)

¹⁶ The (*Holy*) **<u>Spirit Himself testifies with our spirit</u>** that we are children of God,

Dr. Frank Matera's interpretation of this verse spells out my point clearly.ᵛ

"I have rendered the Greek verb *symmartyrei* as "testifies with" because Paul seems to imply that there is an inner dialogue between the believers spirit, which has been transformed by God's Spirit, and the transforming Spirit of God, both jointly testifying that the believers are truly God's children."

So what are we to do according to our human spirit?

Romans 12:1-2 (NASB)

¹ Therefore I urge you, brethren, by the mercies of God, to present your bodies (i.e. *human spirit that has the capability to do both good and evil*) a living and holy sacrifice, acceptable to God, *which is* **your** spiritual service of worship. *(Because you are offering your human spirit for good to God.)*

The human spirit is self-centered. Its self-centeredness is the source of sin and evil in the world as we can see from the first sin described in Genesis.

Genesis 3:4-5 (NASB)

[4] The serpent said to the woman, "You surely will not die!
[5] "For God knows that in the day you eat from it your eyes will be opened, and you will be like God, knowing good and evil."

It is only through the indwelling of the Holy Spirit that we can offer our human spirit to God and transform our minds to His will.

If you don't believe, you are operating from your human spirit. You may hear God's call, but as Augustine's life shows in his "Confessions", you have not yet received the Holy Spirit and therefore sin as a result of the conflicts in your human spirit. When you do receive the Holy Spirit everything changes. The inner dialogue between the Holy and human spirit transforms the human spirit over time as it did for me as described in this book.

Where do we get our human spirit? How does sin rule our human spirit? To answer these questions we need to explore God's purpose for creating us.

2. Understanding God's Purpose For Us: Wouldn't everyone like to understand the ultimate purpose of his / her life here on earth. While no one can comprehend the mind of God, I believe that we can begin to understand the answer to this question in part by focusing on the **one thing God can't do**.

Love is the one thing that God cannot make us give Him because love is only real if another gives it freely and sincerely. In order for God to receive love, He must seek a personal relationship with free individuals. If people turn away from God, God's only recourse is to let them turn away and suffer the consequences or the result of turning to God would not be love.

The first question you might ask is, "if there is a God, what is the result of my disbelief?" Here is what Paul has to say:

Romans 1:20-25 (NASB)

[20] For since the creation of the world His invisible attributes, His eternal power and divine nature, have been clearly seen, being understood through what has been made, so that they are without excuse.
[21] For even though they knew God, they did not honor Him as God or give thanks, but they became futile in their speculations, and their foolish heart was darkened.
[22] Professing to be wise, they became fools,
[23] and exchanged the glory of the incorruptible God for an image in the form of corruptible man and of birds and four-footed animals and crawling creatures.
[24] Therefore **God gave them over** in the lusts of their hearts to impurity, so that their bodies would be dishonored among them.
[25] For they exchanged the truth of God for a lie, and worshiped and served the creature rather than the Creator, who is blessed forever. Amen.

If we look closely at this scripture we see that Paul is telling us that we can see what God is like by observing his creation and His acts. Notice he did not say that we needed to believe a particular doctrine.

If we do not turn to God and instead set ourselves or other things as our focus, then God gives us up to the idols that we have created. Why would a loving God leave us on our own? Why would God back away from us? Why not just keep us on track, make the miracles we pray for happen, and make the world wonderful if he really exists? The answer is that God loves us and wants us to love Him. He gives us free choice to come to him or turn away. If we turn to Him he has the power to justly forgive us through the death and resurrection of Jesus Christ, God's sacrifice for us. If we turn away, we are on our own. This results in some people thinking that God is vengeful and punishes us. The reality is that God simply does not save us from ourselves and the evil around us unless we turn to Him. God's response to our disbelief is to love us and back away.

Why does God want us to love him? I think that God has a plan. I propose the following: God is spirit and He is creating a spiritual family for Himself from those who love him here on earth. While being "born again" has taken on the meaning of receiving Christ into our lives by some of today's churches, I don't think that is all that the Apostles John and Paul are talking about.

John 3:5 says: "That which is born of the **flesh is flesh**, and that which is born of the **Spirit is spirit**". This is specifically saying that we, as individuals, must at some point be literally born in the spirit (not the flesh) if we are to be His children.

Genesis says that God starts by creating the Heavens and the Earth. Later He creates man and woman. We are told that men and women are created in God's image. (We have a spirit and a physical form like Jesus). However, we not only resemble Him, but God has created us so that we can also reproduce. The man's sperm impregnates the woman's egg and another human being is formed. That human being is "begotten" by two humans and has its own physical body and, in addition, a human spirit from its mother and father. I propose that the human spirits of the mother and father join to form the human spirit of their baby. I propose that each of us is the result of the combining of the physical **and spiritual** "DNA" of our parents. This human spirit has the free will to seek God or turn away as described above.

My hypothesis of God's plan for creating us: I propose that the human spirit is the spiritual egg of a spiritual person. From a human spiritual perspective, we are all females. If a person seeks God, God impregnates their human spirit with the Holy Spirit to form a spiritual person, like the father's sperm impregnates the mother's egg to form a physical person. Under this hypothesis, the two spirits (God's and the individual's) become a **spiritual embryo** and eventually are actually born as a spiritual person, a child of God at the time of a person's physical death. If you think back to the story of the Virgin Mary we see this described, in part, in the birth of Jesus.

> **Luke 1:35 (NASB)**
> 35 And the angel said to her, "The Holy Spirit will come upon you, and the power of the Most High will overshadow you; therefore the child to be born will be holy; he will be called Son of God."

Jesus did not have a human spirit because Mary was a virgin. She had to be a virgin under this hypothesis and she was. Human spirits only result from the union of human parents. Jesus, therefore, had the full Spirit of God within his human body. He had both a physical and Holy Spiritual body while He was alive on earth. The Apostles saw his spiritual body during His transfiguration. When He was crucified, his physical body passed away and his spiritual body remained. He is the first Son of God.

Under this hypothesis, the spiritual person is born after the physical death of the physical person. We are literally born again in the spirit as a child of God. This would be you with all your memories, skills and abilities yet in a recognizable spiritual body. As Paul says in Romans 8 Verse 23, we only have the first fruits of the Spirit now and are awaiting our full adoption / birth as God's children. This is what baptism symbolizes. This makes us spiritual embryos throughout our physical lifetime and the earth the womb of God. The human spirit has the choice to love God or turn away. If the choice is to love God, then the Holy Spirit comes upon us as he did with Mary and creates a spiritual embryo by joining our human spirit and the Holy Spirit[vi]. In this way, God creates a true loving spiritual family comprised of "children of God" who truly love him. And, Jesus is the first fruit, so we will be like him. Here is what Paul has to say:

1 Corinthians 15:42-46 (NASB)

42 So also is the resurrection of the dead. It is sown a perishable body, it is raised an imperishable body;
43 it is sown in dishonor, it is raised in glory; it is s own in weakness, it is raised in power;
44 it is sown a natural body, it is raised a spiritual body. **If there is a natural body, there is also a spiritual body**.
45 So also it is written, "The first MAN, Adam, BECAME A LIVING SOUL." (*Human spirit*) The last Adam (*Jesus Christ*) became a life-giving spirit. (*Holy Spirit*)
46 However, the spiritual is not first, but the natural; then the spiritual.

Romans 8:14-17 (NASB)
[14] For all who are being led by the Spirit of God, these are sons of God.
[15] For you have not received a spirit of slavery leading to fear again, but you have received a spirit of adoption as sons by which we cry out, "Abba! Father!"
[16] The **Spirit Himself testifies <u>with our spirit</u> that we are children of God**,
[17] and if children, heirs also, heirs of God and fellow heirs with Christ, if indeed we suffer with *Him* so that we may also be glorified with *Him*.

We will be born again as sons of God.

Romans 8:29 (NASB)
[29] For those whom He foreknew, He also predestined *to become* conformed to the image of His Son, so that He would be the firstborn among **many brethren**;

If this theory is correct, the ultimate purpose of our lives is to learn to love God and others, grow in His love, and develop the knowledge, skills, and abilities that we will need in order to play a role as His children in His kingdom. What a fantastic future! We will be part of God's family, ruling the universe that He has created with, through, and for love.

3. God's Laws: There are two kinds of laws that help us to know God, natural laws from creation that can be discovered through mathematics, science and observation, and spiritual laws that can be discovered through reading the Bible and from day-to-day experiences of the Holy Spirit. Understanding the nature of these two types of laws is important for us in order to understand God's work in the world and within you.

Physical Laws of Creation: Scientists are working to discover what everything in the universe is made of and how it works. In 1687, Isaac Newton discovered the basic formulas that describe what our senses show us about the universe. A German physicist, Max Planck, discovered quantum physics and became the founder of quantum theory at the turn of the 20th century. Around the same time, Einstein developed the theory of general relativity. He later published papers on the general theory of relativity, quantum theory, and the thermal properties of light that laid the foundation for the photon theory of light. From that beginning, scientists and mathematicians have made immense strides in defining the basic nature of the universe and perhaps beyond.

What scientists have, in fact, discovered is that there are layers of reality above and below what we see and feel with our five senses. A popular theory for eons has been that if our five senses can't detect it, (like God) it must not exist. Science has now proven this common thought is a misassumption; most of what is true about creation is not directly observable because the components of the universe are either operating at such a large scale or small scale that they are not apparent.

Quantum Mechanics has proven that the fundamental nature of reality at the deepest level is determined by chance. All is uncertain at the smallest particle level until something is measured. The moment you observe a particle the uncertainty disappears.[vii] There are, therefore, firm laws and mathematical formulas that describe everything, but what they describe is not certain. At the smallest level, there is only a probability that matter exists at any point in space-time, yet what we experience is real to us.

Some scientists feel that God is an invention of man's mind to explain things that are unknown. If science could discover what is unknown, then God and faith would not be needed to explain reality. Whatever we may discover to be true, there is always the question of how did this come to be? Saint Thomas Aquinas had an answer in the thirteenth century. He essentially said in his contingency argument; nothing has been discovered that carries with it the reason for its own existence, except God, who identifies Himself as "I Am".[viii]

I can't help thinking about a quote from the Apostle John.

1 John 1:5 (NASB)
5 This is the message we have heard from Him and announce to you, that **God is Light**, and in Him there is no darkness at all.

While this scriptural text has been interpreted as metaphorical, it may also be literal. This quote and the beginning of Genesis both state that light is part of God's nature. Understanding light has resulted in our discovery of quantum mechanics and the building blocks of the universe.

I believe that what math and science has discovered are the basic building blocks that God has used in creation. I believe that this shows us, in part, how God's mind works. The super strings of quantum mechanics and relativity theory are the DNA of physical creation, where biological DNA is the basic building block of life. God is consistent in using fundamental codes to create the universe and life within it. Could all that we know just be a product of chance?

I contend that, it is God who turns probability into reality. What scientists see as probability, is God's flexibility. God used basic codes and laws to create everything, and we are constrained by these laws. God also chooses to be constrained by His laws of creation. However, He didn't constrain His ability to act in His creation by building reality on uncertainty. This is how miracles can happen without mankind being able to prove that God is behind the miracle. If Gods actions could be proven, the universe would appear arbitrary and there would be no need for people to love God through faith. God's plan to create a truly loving family goes out the window if his actions are provable. Without knowing it, scientists may be discovering that God is what makes the physical world real, and our best science and math point to that truth.

Spiritual Laws: God's spiritual law is the law that should guide our spirit and relationship with God. Paul tells us in Romans and his other letters the story of God's plan to bring individuals to faith in God. However, God's spiritual law at the highest level is easy to explain. Paul tells us what we need to do.

Romans 13:8 (NASB)
⁸ Owe nothing to anyone except to love one another; for he who loves his neighbor has fulfilled *the* law.

So love is the bottom line in what God is seeking from us. The Holy Spirit inspires the children of God to live by the Golden Rule.

Changing Your Story: Before reading my book you had a story in your head about God, your religion, and how you should live. I challenge you to change your mental story to include how you think about the church and church doctrine.

Paul helps us to understand and put the Church into perspective in Romans 14:14.

Romans 14:14-15 (NASB)
¹⁴ I know and am convinced in the Lord Jesus that nothing is unclean in itself; but to **him who thinks anything to be unclean, to him it is unclean.**
¹⁵ For if because of food your brother is hurt, you are no longer walking according to love. Do not destroy with your food him for whom Christ died.

God wants you to love Him and others. What Romans is basically saying in these verses is, if **you believe** that doing something is necessary to obey God and you don't do it, you are not showing love to God even if God does not require you to do that thing.

For example, once Israel believed that the Jewish dietary and other practices were what God demanded, they needed to do them to show love to God. One transgression resulted in sin.

So, if you believe you need to be circumcised, or not eat meat, or worship three times a day, or eat fish on Friday to be faithful to God, then you do. However, there is nothing in Paul's letters or God's Ten Commandment law that requires that you do these things to love God. This is where church doctrine can make it more difficult for you to establish a close relationship with God. Christ did not preach a doctrine other than love God and love your neighbor as yourself.

Dr. Frank Matera supports this view in his interpretation of Romans 14:1-12.[ix]

"Those who are strong in respect to their faith should welcome those who are weak in respect to faith since each person acts in accordance with one's own faith in Christ. Moreover, since judgment belongs to God, believers must refrain from judging one another....What ever does not proceed from the conviction of faith, therefore, is sin."

Perhaps you haven't read the Bible and don't know the difference between what Paul proclaims and what you have heard in the church, the culture, and the family that you grew up in. Are you surprised to know that if you work to grow your personal relationship with God day by day, then you are free of the requirement to follow other religious requirements? "The truth shall make you free"[x]. Good works will naturally follow.

This being said, the church is the best way to learn about God and to form a fellowship with other believers that is key to growing your understanding and faith. Your task is to find a church that will help you to mature in your personal relationship with God. We are all on our own personal journey to become children of God, but we need the church and others help along the way.

The scripture above further says that you should be sensitive to others, not judge them and their beliefs if they are practicing what they think they need to do to honor God. We should not do anything that would cause others to sin in their efforts to believe in God. This might also be true of people of different faiths who love God. If everyone put this into practice, there would be no more religious wars.

Finally, I need to share with you the good news!

Romans 8:28-30 (NASB)
[28] And we know that God causes all things to work together for good to those who love God, to those who are called according to *His* purpose.
[29] For those whom He foreknew, He also predestined *to become* conformed to the image of His Son, so that He would be the firstborn among many brethren;
[30] and these whom He predestined, He also called; and these whom He called, He also justified; and these whom He justified, He also glorified.

Your interest in learning more shows that God is calling you to be His son or daughter and you will be heirs, like Christ in God's kingdom.

Experience the Holy Spirit: If you believe the gospel and love God, you can experience the Holy Spirit for yourself. God is concerned about you and He will use the Holy Spirit to transform your life as he has mine. The disturbance in your heart / spirit can be the call from the Holy Spirit.

There are three ways that you can sense the work of the Holy Spirit in your life. The first is to notice your energy level. When either the human or Holy spirit moves you, your energy rises. Think about how your energy changes when you see someone you love or have the opportunity to do something great. You can tell the difference between the energy from the Holy Spirit and the human spirit by testing the context of the energy against the Bible. Are you excited for accomplishing good or getting away with something? The Bible is the spiritual law and the work of the Holy Spirit will be consistent with the Bible. If you are reading a Bible passage and a verse stands out raising your energy level, the Spirit is calling you to look deeper. Feel your energy level. That is how to sense your spirit and God's.

The second way is to look at history and current world events to see God's work across time and His creation. World events today seem to be leading us toward the end times, but that is another story[xi].

The final and most personal way that the Holy Spirit communicates with you can be seen by observing what is happening in the context of your life. God is alive and active in the world through the work of the Holy Spirit. It seems that unlikely coincidences are often God's way of telling us to listen to the Spirit and to search for what He wants us to do. Active listening to the Holy Spirit is an acquired skill and not a singular event. We must actively pray, watch, and listen to the events and people around us.

I have had many personal experiences of the Spirit acting in my life as I described earlier. It is through experiences like these that I grew in my ability to listen to the Spirit. It takes time and an eagerness to learn.

It is Your Decision: You too can experience personal stories that will help you to see the call of God's Spirit in your life, and see how wonderful it is to give yourself to Christ. If you would like to learn more, please read my book, "The Word & The Spirit: How God Speaks to You"[xii]

A Final Insight: There is one final insight that I would like to share with you. Many people ask the question, "but what about all the good people who believe in other religions? If Jesus Christ is the Son of God, would He condemn them all to hell? Do you have to be Christian?" My response to this question is different than you will hear in church because it is the Church's role to bring you to Christ. My response is based on two scriptures from the apostle John.

> **John 10:11-16 (NASB)**
> [11] "I am the good shepherd; the good shepherd lays down His life for the sheep. [12] "He who is a hired hand, and not a shepherd, who is not the owner of the sheep, sees the wolf coming, and leaves the sheep and flees, and the wolf snatches them and scatters *them*. [13] "*He flees* because he is a hired hand and is not concerned about the sheep.
> [14] "I am the good shepherd, and I know My own and My own know Me, [15] even as the Father knows Me and I know the Father; and I lay down My life for the sheep.
> [16] **"I have <u>other sheep</u>, which are <u>not of this fold</u>; I must bring them also, and they will <u>hear My voice</u>; and they <u>will</u> become one flock with one shepherd.**

John 11:49-52 (NASB)

⁴⁹ But one of them, Caiaphas, who was high priest that year, said to them, "You know nothing at all,
⁵⁰ nor do you take into account that it is expedient for you that one man die for the people, and that the whole nation not perish."
⁵¹ Now he did not say this on his own initiative, but being high priest that year, he prophesied that Jesus was going to die for the nation,
⁵² and not for the nation only, but in order that He might also gather together <u>into one</u> the children of God who are <u>scattered abroad</u>.

If we read these two scriptures together, we see that Jesus taught that there are other flocks (other people) that are not of the fold of those who became Christians. These other flocks certainly include the Jews who believe in God (who are not Christians) as described in Revelation Chapters 7:4 and 14:1-5, and every nation as described in 14:6-7. Yet, it is Christ that calls them. John 11:52 specifically says that He is gathering other nations into one children of God who are scattered abroad.

These scriptures were written to tell the world the truth about Christ and that He is the only way to eternal life. However, these scriptures do not say that Christ is limited from calling others that God loves, love Him, and follow His Golden Rule of love even if they are searching for Him through other religions.

From these verses I conclude the following:

1. There is a human spirit in every person.
2. There is a Holy Spirit that God gives to those who love him.
3. There are physical laws of creation and spiritual laws set forth by God.
4. You will have a physical life and a spiritual life after you die if you love God.
5. If you don't love God you will only have a physical life.

6.Christ will call those who have received the Holy Spirit and have been transformed according to His will.

7.Those who Christ calls are born again in the spirit as children of God and will receive eternal life.

8.While other faiths don't recognize this truth, followers of those faiths <u>may</u> also be called by Christ at his return. This is for God to decide. They may be in for a surprise. However, they will only be called because they love God, follow his law of "love thy neighbor", and have the Holy Spirit within them even if they don't realize it in Christian terms.

9.Christ is the Son of God, and the Bible is the word that God uses to speak to us.

10.God has worked through the Jews and then Christians to tell the world the truth of how to have a personal relationship with Him, but God's truth may be bigger than what we know as Christianity.

11.The way for you to become a Son of God and receive eternal life with Him is through faith and growing a personal relationship with God through the Holy Spirit.

12.Finding a church that will educate you and support your spiritual growth is the best way to get started.

My prayer is that you heed God's call and grow in His love through His Spirit.

Thank you for reading my autobiography. My life is actually my testimony of how God and the Holy Spirit can work in your life just as He has worked in mine.

Charles H. Huettner
www.thewordandthespirit.com

GO OUT NOW REMEMBERING THAT

**IN THE GOODNESS OF GOD YOU WERE BORN
IN THE PROVIDENCE OF GOD
YOU HAVE BEEN KEPT TO THIS DAY
IN THE LOVE OF GOD REVEALED IN JESUS CHRIST
YOU ARE REDEEMED FOR PURPOSES UNAFRAID[xiii]**

End Notes

[i] http://www.airpower.maxwell.af.mil/airchronicles/apj/apj01/spr01/kohn.htm

[ii] You can see the latest rendition of the policy at: https://www.whitehouse.gov/sites/default/files/microsites/ostp/aero-rdplan-2010.pdf

[iii] 1 Corinthians 1:23 (NASB) but we preach Christ crucified, to Jews a stumbling block and to Gentiles foolishness, 1 Corinthians 2:2 (NASB) For I determined to know nothing among you except Jesus Christ, and Him crucified.

[iv] This scripture and all contained in this book are taken from *The New American Standard Bible,* Copyright 1995, by the Lockman Foundation.

[v] Frank J. Matera, *Romans,* Baker Academic, 2010 Page 198

[vi] The Holy Spirit impregnated Mary both physically and spiritually where it only impregnates us spiritually; we already have a physical body and human spirit from our parents.

[vii] Heisenberg uncertainty principle

[viii] *Summa Theologica* written 1265–1274

[ix] Frank J. Matera, *Romans,* Baker Academic, 2010 Page 309

[x] John 8:32

[xi] Charles H. Huettner, *Jesus Reveals Revelation,* Booklocker.com, 2012, ISBN 978-1-60145-319-8,

[xii] Charles H. Huettner *The Word & the Spirit: How God Speaks to You,* Booklocker.com 2012 ISBN 978-1-62141-688-3

They are available online, through any bookstore, or my website www.TheWordandTheSpirit.com

CPSIA information can be obtained
at www.ICGtesting.com
Printed in the USA
BVOW08s0925161117
500478BV00016B/472/P